SELECTED POEMS 1969–1992

By the same author

Scotland's Castle (Reprographia, 1969)
Poems (Akros, 1970)
Four Points of a Saltire—with Sorley MacLean, George Campbell, Hay and Stuart MacGregor (Reprographia, 1970)
Despatches Home (Reprographia, 1972)
Buile Shuibhne (Club Leabhar, 1974)
Galloway Landscape (Urr Publications, 1981)
Cnu a Mogaill (Dept of Celtic, University of Glasgow, 1983)
Wild Places (Luath Press, 1985)
Blossom, Berry, Fall (Fleet Intec, 1986)
Making Tracks (Gordon Wright Publishing, 1988)
Straight Lines (The Blackstaff Press, 1991)
Tales Frae the Odyssey (Saltire Society, 1992)

WILLIAM NEILL

Selected Poems
1969–1992

Canongate Press

Textual Note
As this selection comprises mostly English or Scots
poems, Gaelic originals appear in italic type
with English translations opposite.

First published in Great Britain in 1994 by
Canongate Press Ltd,
14 Frederick Street,
Edinburgh EH2 2HB

© William Neill 1970, 1972, 1981, 1985, 1986, 1988, 1991, 1992.

Poems from *Straight Lines* (1991) are included in this selection by kind
permission of The Blackstaff Press.
The Gaelic poems included in this selection were also published
in the all-Gaelic collection *Cnu a Mogaill* (1983).

The publishers gratefully acknowledge subsidy from
the Scottish Arts Council and an award from the Deric Bolton Poetry Trust
towards the publication of this volume.

British Library Cataloguing-in-Publication Data
A catalogue record for this book is available on request from
The British Library

ISBN 0 86241 476 8

Photoset by Servis Filmsetting Ltd, Manchester.
Printed and bound in Great Britain by Bookcraft Ltd, Midsomer Norton, Avon

CONTENTS

FOUR POINTS OF A SALTIRE
Ayrshire Farm	3
A Celtic History	5
The Death of Cuchullain	6
Beyond Killiecrankie	6

DESPATCHES HOME
Ulysses agus Penelope	10
Old Salt	13
Fhear a sheasas air mo lic	14
Mary	14
Crofting Piper	15
Tilleadh	18
Felix Qui Proprius Aevum	20
Nausicaa	24
Beanntan air Faire	26
The Glen o Dry Banes	27
An Connacht	30

GALLOWAY LANDSCAPE
Galloway Landscape	35
Mull of Galloway	35
Covenanter	36
Demodocus	37
The Power of Advertising	37
Seasons	38
Pedagogue	39
Curlew	39
December Evening	40
Captain Jamie's Dogwatch	40
Edinburgh Don 1971	41
Dead Rat	42

Islanders	42
Poet Without Audience	43
Drifter	44
Dead Lion	45
The Down-and-Up Man	46
Spiders	46
Magician	47
Prelude to Winter	47
Sermon	48
Theban Play	49
Experience Recollected	50
Elizabethans	50
Words for Jim Buckle	51
Chance	51

WILD PLACES

Bull	55
Smeuran an Fhoghair	56
Kailyard and After	57
A Walk on the Hill	58
Flies	61
Generation Gap	61
Drumbarchan Mains	62
Arsair	64
Hertsaw	65
Gone for a Soldier	66
Airgead is Ardan	68
Lament for MacGreegor o Glenstrae	69
John Roy Stuart	71
I Remember, I Remember	72
Moorland Pylons	73
Simmer Time	73
The Harnpan	74
Wild Geese	77
Winter Woodland	78

Olympian Decision	78
The Unknown	79
Cumha Bhaltair Cinneide	80
The Auld Grunn	81
Sirens	82
Posthumous Fame	84
Spring Drowning	84
September Sheaves	85
Sheep	85
Man Walking	86
Kierkegaard	86
Spider Story	87
Lark	88
Landscapes	88
Erncrogo	89
Convert	90
Autumn Light	90
Rural Bard	91
History Lesson	91
A Knell for Mr Burns	92
Exile	93
Viewpoint: Lambdoughty	94
Findabar's Song	94
Taliesin: Strathclyde Winter	94
Beach Walking	96
Exodus	97
Second Wedding	98
First Love	98
A Question for Experts	99
Ballant	99
Forced March	100
Drinks	101
Listed House: Stewartry	101
Nursemaids and Soldiers	102
Lochar Watter	102

BLOSSOM, BERRY, FALL

By the River	107
Gull	107
Winter	108
Cat Accident	108
On Carrick Ground	109
High on Drumconnard	110
Lady Recluse	111
Are You There, Mr Punch?	112
Celtic Legend	113
Stillness	113
Celtic Chapel	114
Tracing Your Ancestors	114
Oakwood and Gall	115
Hero's Child 1927	116
Inshore Gale	116
Night Caller	116
Rowans	117

MAKING TRACKS

Marked Passage	121
Sealltainn thar Cluaidh	122
Yonner Awa	124
Sunday School	125
Cocktails From Shakespeare	125
A Faur Cry Frae Auchinleck	127
Fitsides wi a Prood Hizzie	127
Gallowa Spring	128
The Lonely Place	129
On Loch Ken Side	129
Juvenilia Amoris	130
Tromlaighe	132
Obituary for Captain Taikle	135
Three Women	136
Poet's Walk 1796	137

Aik Tree	138
Hielant John 1930	138
Lucretius, Buik Three Sneddit	139
Soldier's Return	140
Solstice	141
Aghaidh ri h-Aghaidh	142
Clarsair	144
Spinnle an Leem	145
Last Race	146
Lang I Bide Eftir the Lave	146
The Choice	147
A Pushion Pen Pistle	148
Wild Hairst	149
Flichterie Wather	150
Pride Maun Hae a Faa	150
The Simmers Pass	151
A Handful of Silver	152
Suibhne 'sa Mhadainn	154
First Keek at a Corp	156
Berries	156
Prudence	157
Crowd Control Duty	158
Feidh	160
Tree Speik	161
Claonaig	166
Stiopall Ulm	168
Kirks Sudna be Ower Braid	170
Stars	171
Inferno	172
Craobhan	174
Grian is Gealach	176
Caochladh	178
Ermine	179
Geoidh	180
Fasach	182

The Sonnet Goloch	184
Feasgar Fann Foghair	186
Anither Blest o Januar Wun	187
The Truer Vision	188
Old Scholar	188
Liam on his Second Birthday	189
Hill and Cloud	190
Minor Operation	190
Carrion	191
High Squadrons	191
Making Tracks	192
Retour Frae the Ceitie	192
Drumlie Day	194
Seascape	194

STRAIGHT LINES

Gillespie's Wood	197
Home Thoughts in the Piazza	198
The Millman	198
Ms Dickinson (1830–1886)	199
Mull Ferry	199
Neil MacVurich's Lost Poems	200
Seal Women	201
Singing	201
So Fair A Fancy	202
Two Black Fingers	203
Unregenerate	203
Wild Things	204

UNCOLLECTED POEMS

Bonnie Arran	207
Poets' Loanins	209

FOUR POINTS OF A SALTIRE

AYRSHIRE FARM

I remember the black chains that hung
on the swee above the fire, and I remember
the men who sat in the farm kitchen;
they wore stout boots, and their hands were no less tough.
They could not read, or would not read
except what they read in the sky, on the moor and the hills
and the noise of ploughshares ripping the winter turf
was a kind of music to them.

The fire was so hot that I could barely thole it
unless I sat with my back against the wall
beside the dresser; the floor was of stone flags
and when someone moved, tackets scraped harshly.
The men smelt of sheep and horses and cattle and sweat
and the steam of sour milk reeked from their dungarees.
They smoked thick twist in cutties of varying length,
spat juicily and watched the sizzle on the hearth.
Below the door a gap let in the air
to feed a fire that fought with the wind in the lum.
Outside, the mud of the yard was frozen
as hard as the rocks of the Firth.

Even though the byre was warm and sweet with milk
and the breath of cows lulled to a munching peace,
I remember how pleasant it was to go into the house
on clattering adolescent boots to take my place
at the long table, to eat with sharp raw hunger
the farls of scone and the roasted Dunlop cheese.

And after that to listen to their talk.
Puberty kept me silent, fearing their country mockery
reserved for boys; I kept my place
like the cringing collie that slunk in from the byre
willing himself smaller to avoid dismissal.

From his tattered chair the patriarch grinned behind silver whiskers,
refusing to yield before the moving century,
He talked of horses and their habits,
denying the superiority of young Gibb's snarling stinking tractor;
drawing their laughter by gloating yet again
on the morning when indignant spanners rang
cold on the withers of Gibbie's iron horse
while his own Clydesdale team threw all their sweating might
against the swingel-trees.

When he was decently interred, the women
freed from his dour refusal to march
with any times but his own . .
bought a new door for the kitchen
ripped out the friendly range,
covered the floor with a composition
resembling raw black pudding;
introduced carpets and cast out old brass lamps,
immured the whitewashed walls in plaster and paper
disguised the wood that had warmed the spine of Burns
and chopped up the dresser for kindling.
Not to make room for something new . .
but just because it had to go.

When I came back a man to this other kitchen
I missed the tattered chair and the roaring fire
of logs that came from birks . . .
and the company, steaming and roaring and spitting on the grate.

I admired politely the carpets and the new fireplace
but I knew I would never be warm in that place again.

A CELTIC HISTORY

I'm tellt the auncient Celts collectit heids
like some fowks gaither stamps,
an gin ye were their guest wad shaw ye kists
fou o their latest prizes.
Nou we're delivirt frae sic ugsome weys
we scrieve lists o the scunnersomely deid
prentit in black and white.
Yon's faur mair hygienic and forbye
ye can get a lot mair in than ye can in a kist.

I'm tellt the auncient Celts focht in bare scud. . . .
Man . . *yon's* a mark o unco determination.
Ye've shairly got tae ken whit ye're fechtin *fur*
tae tak the haill Roman Empire on in yir buff.
Gin they'd taen Hitler, Napoleon and aa the lave
o the born leaders o sufferan mankind
and gart thaim fecht in nocht but their drawers and semmits
yon wad hae been a solid move towards peace.

Gin: *if* kists: *chests* scunnersomelie: *disgustingly* lave: *remainder* gart: *compelled*
semmit: *undervest*

THE DEATH OF CUCHULAINN*

Of no avail the armoured sickle-chariot
its hooks and spikes and cords and gleaming blades
that cut a bloody swathe across the plain.

Neither the loyalty of Laegh
nor the great hearts of horses,
the strength of a hard-edged blade
can combat their deceits.
From withered leaves and puff-balls
they conjure monstrous warriors
to chill the blood of heroes
and make of champions feasts for hoodie-crows.

If you would live till old age
avoid the destruction of dogs
and heed the warnings of washerwomen.

Faith, said Cuchulainn, looking at his guts:
*if I had known that they were made of meat
and not of iron, I would have been more prudent.*

BEYOND KILLIECRANKIE

Beyond Killiecrankie
in this bare glen the eye
follows the hills' sweep to the sky's rim
escaping a desert land
that fosters only sheep.

---

*v. *Compert Con Culainn*

Beyond Killiecrankie
the moor is bare of tartan.
Larachs alone are monuments
to a promised land's improvement.

After Killiecrankie
the poets praised the heroes;
scornfully mocked the cracked and bloody skulls
of those who mouthed their psalms before the fight.

After Killiecrankie
the swaggering tacksmen hot with victory
strolled home to drink their gentlemanly brandy,
leaving the Cavalier to curse
a premature rejoicing
that left the captured field
open to alien progress:
to carpet-baggers, brewers' sons,
genocide masked as religion
and the resurrected psalmsters.

Beyond Killiecrankie
on this bare moorland
there are neither psalms nor slogans:
only the bleating of sheep,
the victors of that battle.

---

larachs: *sites of ruins*

DESPATCHES HOME

ULYSSES AGUS PENELOPE

Sinn a' seòladh o ho rò
àrd a' chuain o ho rò
eadar Scylla is Charybdis
cunnartach ar triall gun teagamh
sinn a' sìor-lùb air a h-àlach
thall thar chuan o ho rò.

Nuair a rànaig sinn gu cala
'n iomadh àit' bu mhòr an othail
Polyphemus mòr aon-shùileach
's a chuid chaoraich anns an uamh
oillteil gus na chuir mi 'n t-sùil às
leis a' bhiorag dhearg on teine
nach mi 'n gille o ho rò.

Thànaig sinn gu eilean Circe
caileag mhallaichte gun nàire
rinn i mealladh oirnn gu tàireil
sgioba coltach ris na mucan
gus na chuir mi fhìn air bòrd iad
duarman 's talach o ho rò.

Uair eile 's iad a' slùgadh Lotos
h-uile fear dhiubh misgeach sùnndach
's mur an robh mi teagaisg stuama
cha bu mhiann leo tighinn dachaigh
's mi gam breabadh o ho rò.

ULYSSES AND PENELOPE

Sailing sailing o ho ro
o'er the wavetops o ho ro
thro by Scylla and Charybdis
dangerous indeed our journey
aye a-bending on the rowlocks
o'er the ocean o ho ro.

Every time we came to harbour . .
many the place we left our mark in:
yon great one-eyed Polyphemus
keeping sheep within a cavern
horrid till I put his eye out
with a stick hot from the ashes—
aren't I the boy, ho ro.

When we came to Circe's island . . .
she's a shameless, cursed hussy . .
did the dirty on us proper,
all the crew behaved like porkers
till I got them back to quarters
groaning moaning o ho ro . . .

Once they got to swilling lotus
every man as drunk 's a tinker . . .
till I got them off the hard stuff
they'd no thought of sailing homewards,
. . . booting backsides o ho ro . . .

Dè a rinn thu fhèin, a ghalad
nuair a bha mi mach air sàile?
Thuirt mo mhac-sa Telemachus
gu robh daoin' a' tighinn air chèilidh
iomadh carabhaidh a' suirighe
o ho rò is ho ro gheallaidh
b'fheàrr leo sin gun deach mo bhàthadh
's mi gun tilleadh o ho rò.

Thuirt thu rium gun d' rinn thu clò-dubh
h-uile bliadhna on a dh'fhàg mi
h-uile là a' fuaigheal 's fighe
gun bhith 'g èisdeachd ris am miodal
h-uile là a' fuaigheal 's fighe
abair fighe o ho rò.

How did you pass the time my lovely
all the time I spent a-sailing?
My own lad there, Telemachus
says that many came a-courting . . .
fancy men all come a-wooing
o ho ro. . .and raised Old Harry
greatly they's prefer my drowning
to my coming home ho ro.

Passed the time, you say, a-weaving
every day since I set sail dear?
Every day a-sewing, knitting . . .
never listening to their coaxing . . .
every day a-sewing, weaving . . .
weaving, say you? o ho ro.

OLD SALT

To start a journey is not always joyful,
yet most would sail again across uncharted seas.
Remember our former voyages, under warm suns,
the smell of salt and timber and all natural savours,
the welcoming smoke beneath the far horizon?
O for a fair wind to drive again
the prow through hissing water.

Not for the shining gold we cruise
these dangerous seas that smile and roar by turns.
We stretch the canvas, tune the strings of cordage,
learn to obey the order of our calling
because we would not have it otherwise.

We seek tomorrow's tidings in bannered clouds
whose tale is hid from those who do not sail.

FHEAR A SHEASAS AIR MO LIC*

The skull that held the songs of climbing and descending
and those long swinging bones that encompassed herds
beneath this obelisk lie in a crumbling city
that cannot echo now the native voice.

In this kirk yard of the Grey Friars
the sweet singer's voice is stopped;
without shame, it seems, occasional compatriots
gape by an epitaph they cannot read.

Fair Duncan of the Songs,
in words and ways they do not understand
you remain uncorrupted.

MARY

Old riddles taunt our grief.
Why should a golden girl
from all our caring take herself out of life?
Why plant so early in her glowing flesh
these coloured seeds that purchase sleep and death?

---

* The inscription on the tomb of Duncan Ban MacIntyre: 'Man who stands on my grave' in Greyfriars Kirkyard.

What waste, a mind so quick
to depart so suddenly from us,
to turn away from our dull common sense,
wander a haunted wilderness on her own.

We can recall her, paused in a different peace,
following the mood of the page,
loving the land where it battled with the sea.

For all the calmness in her eyes, the quiet smile,
her death is an experience that for us
cannot be recollected in tranquillity.

CROFTING PIPER

Because, at home, by turning a switch
he can hear the drip, drip, drip
of the Saxon natter-torture
twisting his mind out of a Gaelic compass,
in the evening under this falling sun,
free from the hoodies who try to drag his soul
towards their useless virtues,
MacCowal treads the machair by himself,
marks out the ground and doubles it again.

Now in these dying days when all pride grows thin,
whisky cannot be had, gaugers are many and the money scarce.

Skilled fingers, heart and breath,
ivory, blackwood, leather:
the chanter sings to the drones beat.
Hiharara hihorodo
ring out again the ancient *Bells of Scone*
sobs for the *Lost Children*,
or bellows-blast a rippling *Flame of Wrath*
to set Patrick squinting again.

Too long, Too Long (we are by far) *In This Condition*.
The righteous look down their noses,
the baffled tourist grins
as MacCowal bears the treasure of Boreraig
under his oxter, chinking out the coins
of *siubhal, tuarluath, crunluath,*
crunluath breabach, crunluath a mach:*
a kind of gold that in this sunken time
pays up the interest due on history's usury.

---

* Terms for fingering techniques.

TILLEADH*

*Is cuimhne leam
an dèidh nan làithean fada fiadhaich air sàile,
machair uaine Srathcluaidh
sìnte fo bheannachd na grèine
agus beanntan uasal òirdheirc Earraghaidheil.*

*Am fear nach deachaidh riamh thar chuan
cha tig 'na fhradharc an sealladh ud as bòidhche:
tonnan a' pògadh tràighean geal' a dhùthcha,
faoileagan a' sgreadadh gu h-àrd mun chaladh
a b'aithne dha 's e òg,
's an ceò ag èirigh bho theintean aoidheil a dhaoine.*

---

* *Sgrìobhte nuair a dh'fhalbh Stiùbhart MacGriogair gu Siamaica.
Chaochail e air an eilean sin.*

RETURNING*

I remember
after the long wild days at sea,
the green machair of Strathclyde
stretched under the blessing of the sun,
and the noble splendid mountains of Argyle.

The man who has never crossed the sea
will never have that most beautiful sight come into his vision:
the waves kissing the beaches of his homeland,
gulls screaming loud over a harbour that he knew when young
and the smoke rising from the hospitable fires of his kinsmen.

---

* Written on the departure of the poet, Stuart MacGregor, for Jamaica. He died on that island.

FELIX QUI PROPIIS AEVUM

(Bho Claudian)

Is sunndach esan a chuireas seachad a bheatha
air a chroit fhèin bho bhreith gu bàs gun fhàgail,
a chuireas a chudthrom air bata air an aon dùthaich
far am b'àbhaist dha bhith an uair a bha e 'na bhalach,
a' caitheamh gach bliadhna gu sìtheil taobh a chachaileith
gun chuibheal an fhortain ga tharraing gun tròcair air falbh.

Cha robh aige ri òl
'na choigreach bho fhuaran choimheach;
cha deachaidh a chur air chrith
mar mharaich' air oidhche mhòr-ghailleannaich,
no mar shaighdear roimh uchd-bhuailt
nuair a dhùisgeas sgal na pìob' e.

Cha do dh'fhuiling e riamh
deasbadan sgaiteach na cùirte;
chan eil cùis aige sa' Chathair,
chan fheum e idir dhol ann,
ach tha e a' mealadh an t-seallaidh as gloine den speur.
Is cuimhne leis gach bliadhna,
a treabhadh, a cur, a buain,
chan ann a-rèir ainm pròbhaist no prìomh-mhinisteir.
Is aithne dha foghar an eòrna
's an t-earrach duilleagach uaine.

Happy is he who passes his life
on his own croft from birth to death without leaving
who puts his weight on a stick in the same country
that was natural to him in his boyhood
spending his life peacefully beside his gate
without the wheel of fortune drawing him ruthlessly away.

He does not have to drink
as a stranger from foreign springs
he does not have to tremble as a sailor on tempestuous seas
or as a soldier in the breast of battle when the pipe stirs him.

He does not ever suffer
the sneering disputes of the court,
he has no interest in the City
and has no need ever to go there,
but enjoys the sight of the clear sky,
he remembers every year by the ploughing, the sowing, the harvest
not the names of provosts or prime-ministers.
He knows autumn of the corn
and the leafy green of springtime.

Mar a chì a cheart raon a' ghrian
a' dol sìos is ag èirigh a-rithisd,
tomhaisidh esan gach là,
le gach dleasnas as èiginn dha dhèanamh.
Chì e a' choille a chuir e,
is iad a' fas aosda le chèile,
oir b' aithne dhàsan an darach
an uair nach robh ann ach a' chnò.

As the same field sees the sun
go down to rise again
he will measure each day
by each chore that he must do.
He will see the trees that he planted
as they grow old together
for he was acquainted with the oaktree when it was but an acorn.

NAUSICAA

'*A ghruagaich òig an òr-fhuilt bhuidhe
co an duine tha 'nad dheoghaidh?
le coltas air mar mharaiche?*'
'*Fhuair mi esan air an tràigh!*'

'*C'àite an d'fhuair e 'n deise spaideil?
Cha bu shaor a leine geal . . .*'
'*Thug mi deise m'athair dha
is theid e dhachaidh leam gun dàil!*'

'*Phòsadh iomadh fear an eilein
nighean tocharach dhe do sheòrs';
nach feàrr leat duine comasach
seach seoladair a chaill a chùrs'?*'

'*Cha d' fhuair mi tairgse bhuapa fhathast;
cha bhi mi beò air fiughair a mhàin.
Carson a thilginn air àis
cothrom thanaig le muir-làn?*'

NAUSICAA

'Young maiden of the yellow-gold hair
who is the man following you
who looks like a sailorman?'
'I found him on the shore!'

'Where did he get that smart suit?
His white shirt wasn't cheap . . .'
'I gave him my father's shirt,
and he'll be coming home with me right away.'

'There's many a man of the island would marry
a tochered lass like yourself;
wouldn't you prefer a capable man
rather than a sailor that went off his course?'

'I haven't had an offer from them yet,
and I can't live on hope alone.
Why should I throw back
a chance that came in with the tide?'

BEANNTAN AIR FAIRE

*An uair a bhios an oidhche glan, soilleir
chì mi bho 'n fhàrdach seo air Galldachd Lodainn
taobh thall na h-Aibhne Duibh, na beanntan àrda;
chì mi na Tròisichean mar barrabhallan air faire,
am bòidhchead gorm a' streapadh iarmailt an fheasgair.
Chan eil Gododdin an-diugh ach 'na mac-talla an inntinn sgoileir,
ach mur eil Somhairle no Eòin fhathast am Fionnlagan
tha Alba beò air tràighean a' chuain shiar.*

*Fo ghrian òirdheirc an fheasgair tha m' inntinn a' gluasad;
bu mhiann leam èirigh mar Shuibhne an riochd eòin,
ach chan eil mi idir cho mallaichte no cho beannaichte ris-san;
chan eil geimhlean air m' aobrannan gam chumail an seo:
cuiridh mi am màireach m' aghaidh ris na beanntan ud
is a dheòin no a dh' aindheoin fàgaidh mi Lodainn 'nam dhèidh.*

*Ach chan fhada nis gus am bi a' ghrian air dol fodha
is bheir an dorchadas dhòmhsa leisgeul mo ghealtaireachd.*

MOUNTAINS ON THE HORIZON

Whenever the evening is clear and bright,
I can see from this dwelling on Lowlands of Lothian
the high mountains on the far side of Forth.
I see the Trossachs like battlements on the horizon,
their blue beauty climbing the evening sky.
Gododdin today is but an echo in a scholar's mind,
but if Somerled and John are not in Finlagan,
Alba still lives on the shore of the western sea.

My mind moves under the splendour of the evening:
I wish to rise like Suibhne in the form of a bird, but I am neither so
accursed nor so blessed as he.
There are no gyves on my ankles to keep me here:
Tomorrow I will set my face to those mountains
and in spite of all leave Lothian behind me.

But it will not be long until the sun goes down,
and darkness will give me an excuse for my cowardice.

THE GLEN O DRY BANES

Ae day the Twa-Sichtit cam doun the lang glen,
doun the lang glen o the deid dry banes . . .
the deid dry banes that were looms o men
nou liggin hauf-yirdit wi stour an stanes.

---

ae: *one* liggin: *lying* hauf-yirdit: *half-buried* stour: *dust*

An a Voice cam duntin doun oot o the lift
oot o the lift that was toom an bare. . . .
'Wad ye gie the ward gin ye thocht ye'd shift
the hauses an harnpans ye've got doun there?'

'Gin ye thocht ye micht hansel thir bones wi thews
an hap aa thegither wi ticht new skin . . .
an claithe thir auld sinners in plaid an trews . . .
wad ye swall their breists wi a leevin win'!'

An the skreich o the seer on the birlin breeze
Stottit back frae the stany waa's o the glen:
'We hae muckle need o sic chiels as these . . .
thro the yetts o hell I wad cry thaim ben.'

'Thir dreich dry banes here as pouthert as keel
an thir white harnpans that the glaivie split . . .
thir kists that were loused by the dirkies steel . . .
Gin ye grantit the pow'r I wad ettle at it.'

'For ye ken we hae leevin banes eneuch
In bricht new skins happit roun wi claith . . .
but their spirits within are no sae teuch
as thir auld dry banes that want nocht but braith.'

---

duntin: *striking* lift: *sky* toom: *empty* hauses: *necks* harnpans: *skulls* hansel: *give a gift* hap: *wrap* skreich: *screech* birlin: *spinning, whirling* stottit: *rebounded* chiels: *fellows* yetts: *gates* ben: *within* pouthert: *powdered* keel: *ruddle* glaivie: *sword* thir: *these* kists: *chests* ettle: *attempt* teuch: *tough* nocht: *nothing*

28

AN CONNACHT

Thuirt Cromual mu na Gaidheil
'Rachadh iad gu Connacht no gu ifrinn:
cha bhruidhinn iad anns a' Ghàidhlig
taobh an ear dhen t-Sionainn.'

Chunnaic mi an Connacht
achaidhean beaga bochda
taobh a' chuain mhòir;
chunnaic mi an Connacht
crodh ruadh air an reic
air an rathad eadar taighean a' bhaile.

Chunnaic mi an Connacht
creagan is clachan is cladaichean
feannagan is faoileagan is fithichean
is iomadh asal eadar luirgean chairt;
agus leis an fhìrinn innse
chan fhaca mi Gaidheal beartach.

Thug iad biadh is deoch dhomh,
is fhad's a bha mi ag itheadh
bha iad a' seinn 's a' dannsadh
is a' cluich clàrsaich is pìob dhomh
mar gum b' e flath a bh' annam.

An lèirsinn Chromual is dòcha
nach robh difir eadar ifrinn 's Connacht;
ach ged bu Ghàidhlig a chuala mi
taobh an iar dhen t-Sionainn,
chan eil ifrinn ann an Connacht
ach sna bailtean mòra grànda
chaidh a thogail le Cromual 's a leithid.

IN CONNAUGHT

Said Cromwell of the Gael
'Let them get to hell or Connaught:
they won't speak Gaelic
on this side of the Shannon.'

I saw in Connaught
poor small fields
beside the great sea:
I saw in Connaught
red cattle being sold
on the road between the houses of the village.

I saw in Connaught
rocks and stones and pebble beaches
crows and gulls and ravens
and many a donkey between the shafts of a cart
and to tell the truth
I never saw a rich Gael.

They gave food and drink to me
and while I was eating
they sang and danced
and played pipe and harp to me
as if I were a prince.

Doubtless, in the sight of Cromwell
there was little difference between hell and Connaught,
but though it was Gaelic I heard west of the Shannon,
hell is not in Connaught
but in the great ugly cities
raised by Cromwell and his like.

GALLOWAY LANDSCAPE

GALLOWAY LANDSCAPE

I walk on rough thin roads with passing places.

Nobody passes. A grey mist trails its cloak
over dead covenanter and dragoon
shriven of their past quarrels;
prelacy versus presbytery
fires no contention now.
A new, more worldly disputation
has come to boulder and rock,
to compass of cairn and loch.

Now we have learned to worship uniformly;
from the unknowable nothingness
of fissioned atoms
all things should be made new.
Yet some, well-versed in older legends, know
fulfilment cannot come without a sting.
How shall we choose the gift, avoid the aftermath?

The dark hills give no answer.
Prelacy and plutonium are all one
to their uncaring granite.

MULL OF GALLOWAY

In the morning before the mist thickened
I saw the distant peaks of Man and Mourne
framing Moyle's silvered glass.

Later, the creeping fog smelt at the cliff.
The horns roared out a dragon challenge;
a giant answered from the Irish shore.

I meditated on the sad land's extremity.

Returning home at dusk, my isolation came
not from the brown moorland or the flat machair
but that I seemed to travel without mark
towards other headlands more extreme than this.

COVENANTER

They shot Will Graham before his mother's house;
doctrinal dispute: home Calvin, away Cranmer.
Damning and blinding dragoons ignorant of Rome or Geneva
tested his orthodoxy with prayer book and bullet.

Here among summer grass the interest blooms again;
tourists bend double to read the faded glyphs:
for kirk and covenant; now, knowing little of either,
they pause beside Crossmichael's quaint round steeple.

On the dank moss-hags saints and dragoons sleep sound
rolled tight together, blent to a common leaven,
a spark in the heads of those who consider causes,
worry on crucifix, bonnet, knee, confession.

The rest don't care about it. The curious kirk
attracts the eye, leaving the soul unlit.
Bullet and test live on in the mind of God;
the covenanter's cause sleeps as sound as Will.

DEMODOCUS

Just after the President said,
'Gentlemen, you may smoke'
a singer came in, blind and led,
dressed in an odd sort of cloak.

He took his harp on his knee:
with his back against the wall,
plucked the strings tenderly,
started to sing to us all.

An old blind beggar like that!
On the meths as well, no doubt.
But I wasn't entirely glad
when the toastmaster threw him out.

THE POWER OF ADVERTISING

Yon tartan laird in the picter wi his glessfu o whisky
an the bonie pipers playin in yon kid-on Balmoral
cannae possibly be drinkin the selfsame stuff
as yon puir gowk staucherin aboot the Gressmercat
slitterin an boakin his saul oot in the siver
inspired nae doot by bauld John Barleycorn.

Yon dollybird wi the velvet single-en an the hoor's een
puffin et yon lang fag an straikin her lover-boy's pow,
cannae be smokin the same brand as oor Wullie there
hoastin his lichts oot thonner in the Royal Infirmary;
his cough disna ease his kingsize carcinoma
the product o years o research by the cigarette company.

---

boakin: *puking* siver: *drain* hoastin: *coughing*

Man, advertisin, is yon no amazin?
Ye can buy juist aboot onything noo-adays. . . .

Poother tae mak ye whiter,
lipstick tae mak ye ridder,
a hunner assortit smells tae droon oot the stink
o common humanity.

An is it no amazin they've never
made onything, ken, that'll stop ye
deein.

SEASONS

Skeich wes the hert i the spring o the year
whan the weel-sawn yird begoud tae steer
an the plewlan's promise gleddened the ee
atween Balgerran an Balmaghie.

The lang het simmer cam an rowed
the haill Glenkens in a glent o gowd
an the gangan fit on the hill gaed free
atween Balgerran an Balmaghie.

Hairst an the cornriggs flisked i the wun
like a rinnan sea i the southan sun;
then ilka meeda peyed its fee
atween Balgerran an Balmaghie.

Skeich: *skittish* weel-sawn: *well-sown* yird: *earth* begoud: *began* het: *hot*
rowed: *(rhymes with 'cloud') rolled, wrapped up* gangan: *going* flisked: *fluttered*
rinnan: *running* meeda: *meadow*

Nou the lang year's dune, an the druim grows stey
an the snaa liggs caal ower Cairnsmore wey;
the crannreuch's lyart on ilka tree
atween Balgerran an Balmaghie.

PEDAGOGUE

I pace the day before the Young Idea;
hope, in some wise, to teach it how to shoot.
I wonder if within these heedless heads
some spark of wisdom may at last take root.

The message, after all, is much the same . . . . .
'Men must seek virtue beyond wealth and rank.'
I draw my tattered cloak around and think
of my last twenty obols in the bank.

CURLEW

Curlew in the grey light
of the soft summer morning;
curlew on the moor's height
in the light before dawning.

Salt to the memory
like a long mist lifting;
fifty years drop away
in a wild bird's lilting.

---

druim: *hill-ridge* stey: *steep* liggs: *lies* crannreuch: *hoar-frost* lyart: *white* ilka: *every*

DECEMBER EVENING

Last night I came over the hill road from Clarebrand
as the sun dropped low in December's freezing west;
a windless sky held firm the quiet land
and the multitudes of heaven were gone to rest.

Seven layers of hills behind branches naked and black.
Far over Solway thin clouds like golden shells;
the serpent thorns writhed by the empty track
in a silence so still it rang in the head like bells.

CAPTAIN JAMIE'S DOGWATCH

Lost the gold braiding, anchor, rope and crown,
sold into pawn his angled mirrors fade;
white on the gale the lubber gulls sweep down
screaming of mastheads and the Baltic trade.

Many the ports and minds of men he knew.
The wide world's wonders came within his sight;
careened by pain at last, his only view
the city's riding lights against the night.

A foul fluke holds him anchored to his chair,
all distant seas are calm, all far winds still;
caught in the crowsnest of this winding stair
he brings no suns down to his window sill.

EDINBURGH DON 1971

In this high centre
of all that's known and ever can be known
I gaze across the cities of the plain
to clearer skies beyond.

Soon they will come,
secure in their new prophecies,
sure their own causes have the best effects.

Soon they will come, eager disciples;
seeking yearned truths, at last they will come to wisdom,
seeing the years bring no knowledge,
syllogisms no surety.

For my disciples I resurrect no gods,
only the whispering phantoms of old words,
the gibbering ghosts of long-dead certainties.

I am the living link of the old chain,
my cell a little warmer than Lindisfarne,
a little less remote than Icolmkill.

Our faltering guidance still remains unhonoured,
the well-born lackey of the worldly-wise.

I pull my gown around me, close my window
lest in the traitor moment I should hurl
my body concretewards from this high temple.

DEAD RAT

Greatly disgusted, cleaning out a drain
I scooped a limp wet rat up with the mud;
whether through death or the continuous rain
hairless, transparent; I saw bones and blood,

all the fine lineaments of vein and tube.
Eyes smooth as mercury, a polished jade.
Looked for an instant shocked at this foul nude
then threw it from me. Later on that day

in unsought retrospect I gave no grue
of cultivated squeamishness. All I could see
the glass body; within it red and blue
ink lines of most mysterious delicacy. . . .

ISLANDERS

Our longest voyage once
a periplus around the creeks and bays;
there seemed no need or reason for adventure
though some had tempted us with sailors' tales
of long flat isles that lay against the sun,
of mountains black beneath the wing of dawn.
The prophets too spoke of those isles, those mountains,
drove off our pale imaginings with dry laughter,
asking the tellers if their gulls sang sweeter
or if their sea's surge sang a different song.

This was a hard isle, cold and bitter-soiled;
surge of the wave over the gravelled land,
the breeze that came to us over the ocean, clean.
This bounded universe was world enough;
who knows not heaven can be content with earth.

The gulls hovered, fish dried, grain came to sheaf,
year upon year, father to son the plough
and distaff dam to daughter;
our work determined and our leisure scant,
all knowing what was sin and what was virtue;
our prophets told us and we knew the truth.

That was a happy time. We could not know
what later we must learn,
when we were tempted, forced from the mother land,
drawn by the magic over the lying horizon.
In the high towers of the swelling city
our rule could not hold true;
here were strange beasts that we had never seen
flaunting their heraldry to the common view.
Far, far the surging of our singing surf,
far, far the skies, the sure roof of our world,
the herded clouds, bright pastures of our God,
the muted colours of our distant home
drowned by the bronze and gold
that in the market flashed before our eyes.

POET WITHOUT AUDIENCE

He was the last to use our tongue for poetry.
When he emerged, they said, from his secret darkness
he could call from them whatever mood he pleased.

Grown old, we saw him stand in curious places:
the centre of stone circles, mountain sides,
the island woods, the courses of dry streams.

Careless of audience he would declaim his stresses
in sonorous monotones. Sometimes we would creep up
to form an unsought court. He knew our guilt
that all our learning lay in the new words
spoken by all; these he used only, sparingly,
when he required the barest bones of things.

Otherwise he persisted in his eccentricity.

Because he had been honoured by his generation
we applauded loudly when he lapsed to silence,
pretending to understand his different phonology
although he drew no pictures in our minds.

Now, in the city, the scholars pick over his verses
in jealous contention. We tried to make amends,
fixing a bronze plaque to his cottage wall.

DRIFTER

He lived his life as if he had no choice,
to bullying circumstance he raised no voice,
until the day he fell into the river.

Married a girl who happened to be there,
fell quite unwitting into each affair,
until the day he fell into the river.

That day he gasped and gulped and yelled and thrashed,
seeing for once his story plainly flashed
before his eyes that sank beneath the river.

DEAD LION

The prototype of death-or-glory boy,
lucky, you think, to be given a choice of fate
on the clangorous windy plain of topless Troy?
Posthumous fame, or manage the estate.
Forgetting that damned weak spot on my heel,
bathed in the ethos of my bloodshot age
I chose the cheers, being at best a fool.
Misgivings filled me at a later stage.
The glorious name? I'd as soon do without it
though, being dead, I can't do much about it.

Such macho stunts a young man often tries
to win an option on the world's approval.
When Nemesis occasions their demise
the issue's hid from them by their removal.
Take my advice, accept the worst of bosses,
stick to the farm, the office, cut your losses.
Posthumous gongs are hardly worth the wearing.
In Hades, the pale phantom's past all caring.

THE DOWN-AND-UP MAN

Down with your man again
cliff-hanging swine man
watery wine man
and stinking-corpse-hoaxer;
down with your man again
the mudplaster sight man
the weakwidows' mite-man
the crumb-basket coaxer.

But up gets your man again
nail-in-the-wrist man
hole-for-a-fist man
the man-from-down-under;
up gets your man again
the starman, the crown man,
can't keep him down man,
the blow-hell-asunder.

SPIDERS

I cannot love spiders, they seem to me
lacking in moral sense; I will admit
even to their beauty, viewed objectively,
and beautiful are the webs in which they sit.

Their murderous matings fill me with disgust,
carrying female emancipation beyond all bounds
of decency; but their compulsions must
be simply judged on biological grounds.

Yet when they wait, trapped in the bath's bottom,
I brace and succour them before they die.
I deeply know that I am the misbegotten,
rejoicing in the slow death of the fly.

MAGICIAN

Just a plain box, quite empty as you see.
Pick out a card, there's nothing up my sleeve;
to turn fish into men just follow me.
Give them the magic sign? They'll not believe
even if you raise a man up from the dead.
The chances are they'll go away and say
he had a live man stowed beneath the bed.
Corpses don't sleep to wake another day.

But if you make it look like some new skill
of current flowing in a copper spool,
then you may work what miracles you will.
Faced with the mundane every man's a fool.

PRELUDE TO WINTER

Spring was so long ago I can hardly remember
its pains and its pleasures, or at any rate
I'm not bothered much by regrets now that it's ended,
nor hope to retain the urges of that lost state;
gracefully accept, now that the season's late,
the grizzled beard that goes with the grizzled mind;
gladly leave all those foolish gambols behind.

Summer days were the streets' relentless clatter,
office blocks, towering flats and smoky pubs;
far too much beer, much rain and cultural natter,
dancing to the tune of the city's mercantile hub.
Thoughts even of ending it all, but there's the rub.
Trying to look at the state of the world and nation
through the vinous mist of lunchtime conversation.

Now the rowan's red again, the summer's fading,
the sun declines in long autumnal rays.
In a quiet glen I study the distant shading,
wondering why I so foolishly wasted my days.
The spring and the summer cannot be made to stay
but eternity can be caught in the silence here.
The prospect of winter is hardly a matter for fear.

SERMON

He did not know what to say to them:
lying that night, neither asleep nor waking,
remembering the blank sheets upon the desk.
Quotation ranged the corridors of his mind;
considerable learning mocked him in the small hours.

On the eaves the swallows
sang to the summer dawn.
He rose, looked from the window to the gloried east
and shouted silently in the still peace
his heart's praise to the hammered shield of the sky
gleaming on God's right arm.

I will tell them this, he thought.

But as it drew near noon,
looking on the pews,
words could not be found
to tell them that the sun had risen again.

Gathered under the lych-gate
they said to one another,
his sermons grow less keen as he grows old.

THEBAN PLAY

Shepherds hired hurriedly for infanticide,
soiled by compassion, always botched the job,
supplying seed for future patricide,
self-mutilation and the matron's sob;
if she had known exactly who it was . . .
if at the time someone had only said . . .
they'd never have got into the same bed.

What precept comes from all this gore and incest?
Sit in the audience grievously aware
that very little turns out for the best,
that you can't really wake from the nightmare
of certain tragic flaws that we all share.
The idea of living happily ever after
should tickle us to a most cathartic laughter.

The buskin fits life better than the sock.
Though your own hubris goes as yet unchecked
call no man happy till the burial plot.
There's time for you to see the stage bedecked
with carefully random corpses; don't expect
your share of woe to be supplied by art.
The natal sob: cue for your lines to start.

EXPERIENCE RECOLLECTED

The traveller said: I spent some quiet years
among the ruined people in the hills.
Charmed though I was to hear that singing tongue,
behind calm faces I discerned their fears
of that loud knowing mockery that kills
the simple songs their race has always sung.

I saw the ghost their every thought became
in the deep shadows dwelling in their eyes;
from all their hopes I saw the substance fade.
Sometimes they thought upon an old brave name;
then for an instant flickering pride would rise –
flash like a sunbeam on a fighting blade.

Spent by the dullness of this eager place
I try in quiet hours to hear again
their soft and well-knit words from the long past,
search inwardly for some remembered face
to draw my heart up from this busy plain
back to my near-forgotten hills at last.

ELIZABETHANS

With doublet, hose, and secret-fisted sonnet,
poniard in belt and nose to pomander,
high-dudgeoned Ferrara, gesture of cloak and bonnet,
discovery tearing the fixed world asunder,
flaunting of farthingales and inkhorn reason,
rackings for secret Popery and treason;

Teddy suits, blue jeans, small books of chopped-up prose,
judo, karate, macho scents for men;
the secret switchblade, the gig where anything goes;
no bounds on exploration where or when;
bravado that hides an inner perturbation.
The Bomb and the peaceful demo and radiation.

WORDS FOR JIM BUCKLE

Two met head-on and Jim Buckle fell out of the sky;
on a warm desert day he mixed his grains with the sand . .
not in anyone's war: dummy runs in an alien land,
the very last place poor Jim expected to die . .
enter the fell sergeant's mess not reasoning why,
though the whole operation had been most carefully planned.
Who was to know they would try a trick that was banned
by clever commanders to brash young men who fly?

They filled poor Jimmy's coffin up with stones,
symbol of death for when they played the last boast
to keep the books straight as befits the milit'ry code.
The headstone's lying that marks out where his bones
ought to be buried. I know this more than most,
crushed by his coffin's weight on the cemetery road.

CHANCE

They've captured a mutated monkey,
they're teaching the creature to type,
to patter out Hamlet or Timon of Athens
and prove their hypothesis right.

The lines of the cerebral cortex
all answer their calls by a fluke,
though the telephone company looked for a chap
who could follow a technical book.

The shell's equiangular spiral
was not an intended design,
but I'll give you a dose of the copyright laws
if your verses sound vaguely like mine.

Jan Kepler's laws and Ike Newton's
were exceptions proving the rule;
who thinks constellations were planned for their stations
is obstinate, blind, or a fool.

For the universe happened by chance, folks . . .
every scrap of creation's affairs;
for planet and star they are where they are
as chessmen jump on to their squares.

WILD PLACES

BULL

The black bull grumbles at me as I pass,
glossy in noonday sunshine, lashing flies
from his tight rump, and rolling his small eyes.
His nose ring marks him of a higher class
than eunuch brethren of the bullock mass
to whom ungoverned lust for beef denies
the tyrant urge that in his members lies.
His flesh is fire and grass to their mere grass.

In this red heat, none of his munching wives
flaunts her desire beneath his wrinkling nose.
He growls and stamps beside the drystone dyke
to put us all in terror of our lives.
But the wall's firm enough. I stop and pose,
a coward matador to his trapped might.

SMEURAN AN FHOGHAIR

*Is iomadh bliadhna chaidh seachad
bhon a leig mi dhiom geimhlean na h-òige.
ach an diugh fhein taobh a' chnuic
spìon mi smeuran an fhoghair
is ruith an sùgh purpaidh air mo bhial.
Chuimhnich mi smeuran eile,
is gu h-obann, bilean eile.*

*Ach an sin dh' aithnich mi
cha robh caochladh air bith
eadar smeuran an diugh 's an dè
oir tha e ceadaichte dhuinn
am blasadh aig an aon àm.*

THE BERRIES OF AUTUMN

Many a year has gone past
since I cast off the fetters of youth.
But this very day beside the knowe
I plucked the berries of autumn
and the purple juice ran on my mouth.
I remembered other berries,
and suddenly other lips.

But I realised then that there was no difference
between the berries of today and yesterday
for it is allowed to us to taste them at the same time.

KAILYARD AND AFTER

When I wes wee I hud tae dae ma share
mulkan the kye wi the weemin in the byre;
I mind hou I wad scoosh lang streemin jaups
that loupit in the luggie makkin froth
rise oot frae yon rich deeps.

The douce kye skelpit roon thaim wi their tails
tae dicht the flees aff; whiles they'd cotch yir lug
a fair bit ding: ye'd sweir ablo yir braith.
An whiles the wilder yins wad try tae pit
their fit intil the luggie an caa ye oot
on tae the settles, luggie, stuil an aa. . . .
an gin ye didna sett in ticht eneuch
there ye wad be, rubbin a sair hainch
a loch o mulk aboot ye in the grup,
the auld dug barkan an the weemin lauchan

---

luggie: *milk pail* grup: *drainage channel* sharn: *cowdung*

tae see yir breeks aa smoort wi mulk an sharn.
Man, whit a contrast tae ma life-style nou . . .
nae dungarees, nae luggie and nae kye.

Escape to the tailored suit,
the pan-loaf speech,
the benefits of higher education,
the dull rewards of strict conformity.

O what a fall was there, my countrymen.

A WALK ON THE HILL

Walking the hill's the only thing worth while
after the Sunday papers, London style
journalism that tries to take the place
of vanished rituals, but lacks their grace.
It is not likely that the great will care
for old men's brooding over things long gone:
old faiths, old tongues, the runes we leaned upon.
Grazing sheep are the only audience here.

Wordsworth wandered under wheeling plovers,
boomed behind trees to frighten rural lovers.
He knew the ghost that lived in rock and thorn,
could not escape the groves, being druid-born.
We do not have his audience to share
his cadences, start from his common ground
to sense the deeps that lie beneath the sound.
Where are they now who once had ears to hear?

---

kye: *cows*

They are hard at work on urban confrontation
at levels fitting to their rank and station,
not to be seen here in this empty land
of sloping rigs, hawthorn on either hand.
In my lone head I hear the antique reasons
for sky and water, rock and thorn and cloud,
the road that leads from naked birth to shroud,
flesh divided into seven seasons.

Each seven years they say a man's renewed
from head to toe. With what are we imbued
that holds our dying substances in one
from our first suck until the whole thing's done
and all our dust and moisture split and spread?
Some secret otherness than flesh and bone
that links the child to age when cells are gone:
the hidden ghost of soul and heart and head.

Alembic to electron microscope,
in all their science not a meagre hope
that they can formulate the unseen mist
that into our more solid flesh is pressed;
a shade no man-made gear can mark or trace,
a flash caught only in the mystic mind
when reason's calculation's left behind;
for there's no law or logic fits the case.

The ram that moves within the thicket there,
covers his mistress with no courtly air.
A mouth and bowel motion: oestrogen
dictates his lust. Unlike the way of men
who of their procreation make a game
played out in joy or pain as falls the case.
With no more eye towards the future race
we give the ram's task a poetic name.

The beasts that move upon the hillside here
are moved by herdlife, hunger, lust and fear.
I wonder all cannot see man's clear case
lies beyond this poor gift in granted grace.
It is the moving spirit that makes man
the sole possessor of clear thought and choice:
arrangement, pattern, altruism's voice,
great art and memory and soul and plan.

In fleshly procreation egg and seed
march down the centuries to make the breed,
but we are bound by other, unseen chains,
for when the bone is dust, this wraith remains.
Today I walk in step with it on the hill,
the unseen footstep of another walker
who fills the silence with a kind of talking.
When I am coffined, I may walk here still.

For it is not mere flesh, mere blood and bone
crushes this grass and stumbles on this stone,
but all things linked to one, yet separate;
a one-not-one with a much greater state
in which upon this hill I join and part
as the mind fills and ebbs with every step.
By rock and root and drystone dyke and slap
the stillness of true knowledge fills the heart.

Now in still hope down from the hill again,
back to the weary cities of the plain
that in their complications ape the beast,
make, for all knowledge, false gods of the least.
Traherne knew all about the Landlord's will:
the great heritage that stretches to the rim
of vision or the reach of willing limb.
All that's worth while is walking on the hill.

FLIES

Scenting my sweat run free in the still heat
as if I were a corpse the flies buzz round;
by them, it seems, no difference is found
between my flesh and the moor's carrion meat.
Mutton's a mere knife-edge beyond the bleat
and death a subtle absence of all sound,
a change from just above to under ground
where none are snubbed or favoured by the leet.

Still, the road's grand under this July sun
that tans my hide as tough 's a leather purse.
Though flies and sweat give rise to graveyard thought
perhaps I'll make it till this long day's done.
Maggots can wait until my meat turns worse
than it's gone yet under my lifetime's rot.

GENERATION GAP

Doubtless when he bent down to pick up
pebbles, and to snatch a quick look round,
he heard the old men growling: *Cheeky pup*,
seconds before Goliath hit the ground.

So, son, the day you undertake
the local giant's precipitate removal,
do it, by all means, for society's sake.
But don't expect your Dad's help. Or approval.

DRUMBARCHAN MAINS

There's monie a nicht I sate in the ingle-neuk
up et Drumbarchan whan I'd taen ma fee,
the rettlin wunnocks jinin in the crack. . . .
ye cud hae yir telly onie day fur me.

Tae faa asleep in yon bothie, bien and quait
binna the auld meer champin her yeukie heels.
I needit nae het hap tae warm ma feet
nor peels fur a lown belly eftir meals.

Nou there's nae horse tae be fund aboot the ferm
but a muckle rid tractor ahint the stable door
syne auld-sons frae their faithers needna learn
tae ken the fur-ahint frae the lan-afore.

Yince I gaed back tae tak a letter there;
the wife hersel wes loupan roon in breeks. . . .
no dungarees, ye ken, but velvet claith. . . .
her dowp wes gey near burstin thro the steeks.

The youngsters tell me that I'm no jist wice,
tae girn at progress, but there's ae thing plain:
Drumbarchan. . . . Goad! I dinna ken the place. . . .
hell mend me gin I gang yon gate again.

---

taen ma fee: *been hired* rettlin wunnocks: *rattling windows* jinin in the crack: *joining in the talk* binna: *except* meer: *mare* bien an quait: *comfortable and quiet* het hap: *heated blanket* yeukie: *itchy* peels: *pills* lown: *free of wind* steeks: *stitches* auld-son: *eldest son* loupan: *jumping* dowp: *backside* fur-ahint, lan-afore: *positions of horses in yoke* yince: *once* wice: *wise (rhymes with 'dice')* girn: *complain* ae: *one ('yay')* gang yon gate: *Go that way* gin: *if (hard 'g')*.

ARSAIR

*'Na mo sheasamh an seo ag amharc air cuithean
'nan laighe fhathast air taobh Meall Liath
is sneachd mar chrùn ri maol a' Chùirn,
tha ainm gach taigh is cnuic 'nam inntinn,
mar chagar failteach beul Tìm.*

*Is gann a tha fios aig an fhear seo
is e tionndadh chlais le tractair,
air ainm an aite aige fhein
ach mar fhuaim neònach 'na chluais.*

*Agus nam bithinn 'ga theagaisg,
dh'eisdeadh e le foighidinn
ri cabaireachd a' bhodaich
mun do chuir e sios a chàs,
a' sporadh eich gun mhathair
air falbh bho a leithid de sheanachas.*

*Tha cròdh na mointich a' coimhead orm.
Is uasal an sloinntearachd acasan,
is tha iad a' geumnaich gu h-àrd
an cànain an sinnsre.*

ANTIQUARY

Standing here, looking at the drifts
lying yet on the side of Millyea,
and the snow like a crown on bald Cairnsmore
the name of every house and hill is in my mind,
like a welcoming whisper in the mouth of time.

This fellow here does not know,
and he turning furrows with a tractor,
the name of his own place
except as a curious noise in his ear.

And if I were to teach him
he would listen patiently to the greybeard's gossip,
before he put down his foot
to spur his motherless horse
away from such chatter.

The moorland cattle watch me.
Noble is their ancestry,
and they bellow loudly
in the tongue of their ancestors.

HERTSAW

Ye're a byornar scunner
deleerit and rouch,
stauchran hame et midnicht,
faa'n doon i the sheuch.

———————

Hertsaw: *Heart balm* scunner: *object of disgust* stauchran: *staggering* sheuch: *ditch*

Whit fur ye're no coortin
wi an ee tae get mairrit
on the dochter o yon fairm
wi nae sons tae inherit?

Yon yin thet refuised ye
has aidled yir harns;
tak saw fir a sair hert:
kye and weel-biggit barns.

The morn whan yir heid stouns
and dings lik a smiddy,
tak tent whit I tellt ye
and wad muckle Biddy.

GONE FOR A SOLDIER

I came from what they thought a godforsaken region
high among barren rock and mountain manners.
They grinned when I sought to join their famous legion
with its drums and armour plate and hoisted banners,
miniscule pay, sour drink and pigsty dinners.
But I was mad for some way of escape
from high unending hills and the herding of sheep.

---

harns: *brains* kye: *cows* stouns: *thumps* smiddy: *smithy*

I never thought, seated on long hill slopes
that there could be a way of life even duller than that;
who had assumed it beyond my highest hopes
to get down from the climb, walk easy on the flat
fertile cornland. A tribesman forever caught
in the endless breeding-cycle of the herd
and the gossip of men without polish in their words.

I found nothing here but high noses and stiff spines
on the promoted lowly and the privileged high,
teaching the yokel blockheads to form lines,
to trail and to port, to stand to and stand by,
to fasten a web of straps in the proper way.
From a free man among shepherds I became a slave
caught in the relentless clan of the mindless brave.

So now, when not stamping about in the steely eye
of that tough shining veteran with the acid smile
or sweating under gear, aching in shoulder and thigh,
trudging in hard boots mile after thirsty mile,
my heart yearns for the hills, for the rocky defile,
the bleat of sheep, the rattle of horn and hoof,
and I grieve before sleeping, under an alien roof.

AIRGEAD IS ARDAN

*Feasgar is mi 'nam shuidhe 'san taigh-òsd
choinnich mi fear a thuirt gur e bàrd a bh'ann.
Thug mi dha drama 's dh' èisd mir ris a bhòsd,
is aodach na bochdainn air bho chois gu ceann.*

*Dh'òl e a shàth, is co ach mise a phaigh e
is dh'innis e dhomhsa le fanaid 'na dhol a muigh:
airgead nad phòc', chan ann ach plaighe—
tha sàr ulaidh eadar mo dha chluais.*

MONEY AND PRIDE

One night as I sat in the inn
I met a man who said he was a poet.
I gave him a dram and listened to his boasting,
and a beggar's rags on him from head to foot.

He drank his fill, and who but myself that paid it,
and mockingly he told me as he went:
money in your pocket's nothing but a nuisance,
I have a real treasure between my two ears.

LAMENT FOR MACGREEGOR O GLENSTRAE

Frae the Gaelic

(The chronicle o the Vicar o Fortingall: 1570. The vj da of Apryill
Gregor MacGregor of Glensra heddyt at Belloch
anno sexte an ten yeris)

Richt blithe upo yon Lammas morn
my luve and I did play,
but my puir hert wi dule wes worn
afore the bricht noonday.

Cursit the lairdlings and their freens
wha brocht me til this grief,
wha cam in traison tae my luve
and twined him lik a thief.

Dule: *grief* twined: *bound*

My een wad neer hae shed thir tears
nor wad thy sire be deid,
gif there had been twal clansmen here
wi Greegor et their heid.

His hause laid on an aiken clug,
his bluid skailt on the grun;
hid I a bicker of yon bluid
fain wad I drink it doun.

Wad my ain sire a leper wir,
Grey Colin seik wi plague
The Ruthven lassie wringan haunds
aside whaur they wir laid.

Grey Colin and Black Duncan baith
sae ticht I'd twine in airns
wi ilka Campbell in Taymooth
weel happit roon in chains.

Upo the green o Taymooth Tour
in wanrest I wad staund,
nae lock unruggit on my heid
nor skin upon my haund.

O gin I had the laverock's flicht
bauld Greegor's virr abune,
the tapmost stanes of Taymooth Tour
I'd caa doun til the grun.

---

hause: *neck* aiken clug: *oaken block* skailt: *scattered* airns: *irons* wanrest: *unrest*
unruggit: *unpulled* laverock: *lark* virr: *strength* caa doun: *knock down*

Their wives are happit snug et hame
sleepan the nicht awa:
by my ain bed I bide my lane
until the daylicht daw.

Fain wad I be wi Greegor there
in muir and birk alane,
than beddit wi the Laird of Dall
in waas o aislar stane.

Fain hud I been wi Greegor
in an orra sark o hair,
than weiran silk and velvet
wi the Laird of Dalach there.

Ba hu, ba hu, my son forfairn
sae weirdless and sae smaa
I fear ye'll tine the tid, my bairn,
o vengeance on thaim aa.

JOHN ROY STUART

My face to the driving rain and my heart colder,
not in the fear of death, or exile from a mortal land;
fairer than this bleak moor the fields of France
where a smooth courtly language flows upon the tongue
in pleasant chateaux of the Loire.

---

happit: *wrapped* muir and birk: *moor and wood* aislar: *ashlar* orra sark: *common shirt*
forfairn: *forlorn* weirdless: *ill-fated* tine the tid: *lose the chance*

Why should the heart yearn
for the drizzling crags of home and the poor hovels
that scatter the heather in the damp mists of the west:
a country of drovers, vendetta and harsh words,
of an old and dying poetry of forgotten heroes
and what in these brown glens or in all Scotland
could buy the elegance of one Parisian street?

Now that the walls of Dunedin of the Kings
no longer are defence, the only battlement
the hedge of my clenched teeth around a tongue
that carries the rough Gaelic of Strathspey.

This is the poor excuse, the last defence
that turns my face to the rain and breaks my heart.

I REMEMBER, I REMEMBER

The house where I was born, a ruin now.
Today I saw it after fifty years.
The window panes were shattered, beams brought low,
the rain running on stone like exile tears.
Strange that an image in the memory wears
a backlit glamour even into age
till truth writes colder history on the page.

Yet memory's bright lie was part of me:
those tumbled doors and walls and rotten stairs
were less a part of my reality
than the long dreaming; the ruin was there
to stun the heart, to lay the ego bare
of false nostalgia laced like armour round
my dying body's muddy-mettled ground.

Poorly remembered house, shade of myself,
as much a ruin as I soon shall be.
Richer or poorer, sickness or in health
full circle brings a neater symmetry
between old age and youth's dead mystery.
The shivered glass, the moss, the fallen slate:
the misting mind beneath the balding pate.

MOORLAND PYLONS

High on the moorland the wind sings through wires
strung on the shoulders of the striding pylons.
What gods were robbed for these Promethean fires
in the tight prison on these iron columns?

Under the giants' feet bog-cotton grows;
sun's greater fire sinks to the distant hill.
Chained fire and free must to some junction flow,
pylon and stalk root in a common will.

SIMMER TIME

Simmer tid again an the whaups whustlan
in the gloamin licht upon the heich grunn,
an my een tak in the haill Wastlan
in the rid licht o the lang sun.

Simmer tid: *Summer time* whaup: *curlew* heich grunn ('ch' hard as in 'loch'): *high ground* Wastlan: *Westland* een: *eyes*

An auld man that sud ken better
nor staun here in a sheuch and gowp
et a wheen whaups an a sun settan.
Whitna thing tae gar the hert loup!

THE HARNPAN

(Taen frae an auld Gaelic tale)

Ae nicht as I wes waakin by the kirk
I spied an oabject liggin in the gress,
roon, white and glaizie lik a muckle baa.
Wi the heuk o ma stick I gied it a rare dunt
fur aa the warld lik drivan aff the tee.
It loupit twa-three yairds and gantit up,
an ugsome harnpan o some ither day.
Hou, said this ferlie wi a thrawnlik hoast
'd ye like yir ain heid skelpit wi a stick?
It seems a bodie canna lig in peace
and jouk the umrage of the leevin warld.

---

sud: *should* nor: *than* wheen: *few* gar: *compel* loup: *leap*

harnpan: *a skull* liggin: *lying* glaizie: *shiny* gantit: *stared* ugsome: *disgusting*
thrawnlike: *surly* skelpit: *smacked* umrage: *spite*

Ye maun forgie me, sir, I trummilt oot
it wisna my intent tae skite yir scaup;
forbye I didna ken et banes could speak.
I thocht the gabs of gaishens wad be steekit.
In onie case, gin I had ainlie kent
juist whit ye wir, the last thing I'd hae din
wad be tae yaise yir harnpan fur a baa
Is there onything, yir grace, that I micht dae
tae see ye yirdit fairly yince again?

Na, na, said he, *I've had eneuch o yon.* . . .
ma een and mooth and neb aa stown wi glaur. . . .
we naither braith nor sicht, lang days an dreich
nichts aye gae by withooten crack or claiver.
Nou, gin ye wad be quat of yon sair skelp
juist tak me hame and pit me on a stab
whaur a kin see and whiles hae a bit blether. . . .
and speak belike a ward whiles in yir lug
fur leevan chiels aye want for guid advice.

Weel, I gaed hame and pit him on a stang
atween twa busses on the gairden dyke.
Aa nicht he maun hae girnt and gantit there
ootbye amang the tattie-rigs and neaps,
but cam the morn the wife cam skreichan in.

Goad! Whit's yon grugous scunner i the yaird?
Is yon a puggie's harnpan on the dyke?

---

scaup: *scalp* gabs: *maws* gaishens: *skeletons* steekit: *stitched* yirdit: *buried* dreich: *dreary* stab: *post* busses: *bushes* neaps: *turnips* skreichan: *yelling* grugous: *horrid* puggie: *monkey*

Weel, I thocht, ye're the wumman that aye thinks
that ye ken mair nor onie ither sowl
but nou, belike, for yince I've bestit ye.
Yon, says I, *is a skelet that kin speak.*
Oot gaed I bauldly wi her et ma heels.

Heh, Maister Langsyne-Deid, says I
wull ye jist shaw this wumman ye kin taak?

He keekit up wi yon fell sleekit smirk,
but not ae single cheep wad he lat oot
seean the wife luk dootsome doon her neb.
She didna say a ward but trintled aff.
Weel, ye'll jalouse, I felt a glaikit gowk.
Whit wey, I said, soorfaced, *did ye no speak?*

Ma wards, says he, *are ainlie fur yirsel.*
Aye syne yon scud ye gied me on the heid
we hae a kin o sibness you and me
we canna hae with onie ither bodie.
I taen the strunts and didna speak nae mair.

Weel, frae yon day, things gaed frae bad tae warse.
I wes no weel and bidit ben the hoose.
Last nicht the doacter whuspert in her lug
in yon douce-drumlie wey the craiters hae
when ye're ayont the pooer o their feesick.
An then, forbye she caat the laayer in
smilan and skailan oot a shaif of blauds,
stechan a pen intil ma wearie nieve.

---

sleekit: *sly* neb: *nose* trintled: *tripped* jalouse: *surmise* glaikit gowk: *silly cuckoo*
scud: *a clout* taen the strunts: *took the huff* douce-drumlie: *calmly serious*
shaif of blauds: *sheaf of papers* nieve: *fist*

Yon skelets herrit me o hale and siller;
Whiles nou she sets him on the chimla-brace
near whaur I yaised tae set.
Syne ilka fornicht whan the hoose is quait
I hear him whusper in his sleekit wey
the while she lauchs and skreichs lik onie wutch.
Gin ma waik shanks wad cairt me doon the stair
I'd dird him neb-doon in the kirkyard glaur.

There's sticks fur kennlan and there's sticks fur gowf,
and here's some guid advice, gin ye'll tak tent:
yaise ilka gibble juist fur whit it's meant.

WILD GEESE

Saved from the north the geese
cry by the wintering loch,
fearless on our thin ice
in a sharp present that's undimmed by thought.

Their sight is not my seeing
by dark water and waving sedge;
closer to all true being
with their strong pinions beating the wind's edge.

---

herrit: *robbed* chimla-brace: *mantelpiece* dird: *plant* glaur: *mud* kennlan: *kindling*
gibble: *gadget*

WINTER WOODLAND

Lonely my walking in the woods,
slow is my step on fallen leaf,
flown from the tree the springtime brood,
the acorn in the earth asleep.

Until spring leaf the branch again,
sun wake the seed from winter's death,
skies brighten after April rain,
lonely I walk the forest path.

OLYMPIAN DECISION

A caterpillar looped across the road,
by dire chance parted from his habitat,
with such a humble creeping motion that
I felt an urge to set up as a god,
ape the Far-Smiter, wield the lighning rod,
a hubris born of neither love nor hate.
I was the arbiter of his small fate:
whether to help him over, stamp him dead
or leave him as he was. I let him go
to struggle onwards to the farther rim
and come by virtue to his motley wings.
Why I such mercy showed I do not know
when inner demons shouted: Flatten him!
Doubtless some hungry bird put paid to things.

THE UNKNOWN

When the unknown began to rattle and bang
immoderately in the empty room upstairs;
when, as if tipsy, it obscenely sang,
they blacked it out with everyday affairs.

The children, young, were balked by fairy tales.
Later, some explanation was required
for manic laughter and demonic wails
that kept them wide awake though overtired.

And pat, when they divulged the family secret,
to their surprise it came as no surprise,
since the children, it appeared, already knew it;
laughed at the guilt in their parents' turning eyes.

CUMHA BHALTAIR CINNEIDE

(1450–1508?)

Chunnaic mi Bhaltair Cinneide
a' coiseachd troimh clach mo shùl
fo sgàil a' Chaisteal Dhuibh
aig am laighe na greine
is grinneal fo chois
air tràigh liath Dhùn Iubhair.

Ach cha robh e an lèirsinn
duine air bith eile;
cha chuala iad a cheum
is cha b'urrainn dhaibh idir
a leabhar a leughadh
ged a shin e sin dhaibh;
chan fhaic a'ghràisg ud
an larach Ghillebhride
ach ballachan falamh
air am bu toigh leò
graffiti ùr a sgrobail
anns a' chànain eile.

IN MEMORY OF WALTER KENNEDY

I saw Walter Kennedy
walking through the apple of my eye
under the shadow of the Black Vault
at the time of sunset,
and gravel under his feet
on the grey beach of Dunure.

But he was not apparent
to any other person;
they did not hear his step
and they could not read his book
though he offered it to them;
that gang could see nothing
in Gilbert's ruin
but empty walls
where they were pleased
to scratch new graffiti
in another language.

THE AULD GRUNN

They laucht whan I cam back tae the auld grunn;
watchan the dominie scart in the wersh yird,
heisan the slabs back on the cowped dykes,
makkin a bing o stanes ayont the heid-rigg.

---

grunn: *ground* dominie: *schoolmaster*

They said: ye'll haurdly grow eneuch fir ane;
ye's get nae siller howkan yir guts oot there;
why sud a man o education try
tae wring his keep oot o yon histy grunn?

Settan lik lairds oan their fancy new machines,
mitherless dreggans breathan the reek o hell,
they keekt et me asklent, girnan tae ane anither
as if I'd taen ma lang daurg-days frae thaim.

But ma ain kin wrocht here, afore they left
the lane broon mosses fir the dowie touns:
this yird wes treisure tae me and its paibles gems,
thir drystane dykes ma castle's curtain wa.

Nou they play lounfu tricks when the daurk hides thaim,
they pit their bairns tae skreichan, cowp my dykes,
they thraw the seeds of dockens in ma corn.
But I hae stellt ma feet, and staun firm till I dee.

SIRENS

Grey Mr Kroisos sit in the mezzanine,
watch the ghosts dancing on the dark sea;
salt in the eyes among cigars and wine
the tears flow back to childhood poverty.

---

howkan: *digging* histy: *barren* daurg-days: *workdays* wrocht: *worked* mosses: *moorlands* yird: *earth* lounfou: *lubberly* stellt: *braced*

Barelegged in the narrow harbour streets,
hungry and supple, tuned by sirocco and sun.
Flesh now corruptly sated with all meats,
ashes and dust are the battles you have won.

Recall again the bloomed and swollen grapes
whose bursting juice fermented your warm youth;
call no man happy till the ultimate
vintage is pressed from the sharp fruits of truth.

Now lost the raven's wing, bold flashing eye,
the first hot kiss of your dear native earth.
In your shrunk heart a zephyr of old sighs
breathes once again remembered peasant worth

against the discards, fat on alimony,
deserted Circes of a passing spell
who rouse at last no lust or charity.
Horns of today's dilemma fit you well

crossing slim legs to plan with slanted eyes
smiling denial of senile vigilance.
Lackeys provoke her list of memories
of brief delights sparked by such happy chance.

The white craft is becalmed in the blue bay.
No need to bid them bind you, stop your ears;
the songs they sing are faded quite away,
evede the summons of both wealth and tears.

POSTHUMOUS FAME

Do poets now at rest in their new mansions
look through the windows of eternity
to view from these Parnassian expansions
their work examined by posterity?

Ah, hear them say, that's not the thing at all
I meant to say the day I wrote the song,
but what I meant to say I can't recall
and even if I could, they'd get it wrong.

SPRING DROWNING

Plunging from the overhanging bough,
the few late seconds of a stripling life
led swiftly to the final knowledge: now.
The cold wounded his body like a knife.

Joying in spring he would not think to go
to sudden darkness as the mirror broke
and loosed him to the winter mountain's snow
that lay in wait beneath the cloven rock.

The thrill of death thrusting through the ribs' cage
to set him gasping in the drumming dark,
to leave them mourning in a grievous rage
the callous smooring of his brief bright spark.

SEPTEMBER SHEAVES

Now I have lost a joy that pleased my soul,
looking from this window up to the long park,
where now the giant combine grunts and rolls
to get the lot done between dawn and dark.

I mind the day when on this sloping face
the golden sheaves stood like a waiting host
stook upon stook; today with little grace
their haste will swallow what my eye loved most.

SHEEP

Sociably munching, a bachelors' club of rams
carry their *raison d'être* between their hams.

Soon they will be divided by their duty:
transmitting the blood-line of ovine beauty

to the next cavorting troop of silly lambs
growing to the seeming end of ewes and rams.

An unvicious circle which seems to have one point:
supplying mankind with a jersey and Sunday joint.

MAN WALKING

On the hill-slope man merges into trees,
loses particular, melts to stone and grass
where following breezes lend him a swift ease
as he strides on past all so all things pass;
all blood and sap beats warmly through one heart,
all sight is gathered to the falling sun;
no leg or stalk or trunk that moves apart,
the sinews of all being move as one.
The vein runs crystal, blood flows in the stream,
blossom on flesh and bush, sky set in gold,
eye that sleeps sound within a waking dream.
True power all motion in his cupped hands hold
in a warm grasp that merges heart and mind,
all separateness turned to a common kind.

KIERKEGAARD

Breeches, however warm, if incomplete
focus the interest of the sniggering plebs.
Dreaming regardless in the city street
the sage wore trousers with uneven legs.

Profanum vulgus simply doesn't care
for the well-tailored thoughts within the head.
Odd trouser legs are much more its affair;
eggheads occasion mirth until they're dead.

SPIDER STORY

Swing spider. So I concentrate my mind.

Food after battle, licking bloody hands.
The southern voice: you eat your countrymen.
Those I had slain shrugged off for rebel bands
fittingly dead for their foul plundering.
Now they seem close to me as my blood kin
who saw as virtue what I took for sin.

In holy sanctuary I sought quiet talk,
cool words to mellow a hot difference.
I could not guess that flaring pride would balk,
swift point stab out to where I saw offence.
A single sacrilegious death unplanned
bids me slay many in the Holy Land.

What wars are evil and what battles just
priests of all armies eagerly debate.
I, who lie cold here, fight because I must.
Vassal repentance has been left too late.
I fight for life and land and if I fall
plead cause alone to the liege-lord of all.

Swing spider. So I concentrate my mind.

LARK

Lark sings as she has always done
over the thorn hedge of the spring meadow.
Now my time's very nearly run . . .
long gone the day of the coarse fellow
who heard the song and indifferently whistled
and thought of beef and beer and fun and girls,
ignoring warnings of his careless heading.

Now Lark has a deal more of attention:
a careful leaning on the broken gate.
I think of the subject we try not to mention,
former abstractions of our certain fate,
cold speculations on threescore years and ten.
Sing Lark, sing Lark to me and then
perhaps the scented hour will seem less late.

LANDSCAPES

Young, I recall standing on a fair shore,
my gaze fixed on an island whose soaring peaks
called to me: *come, this is the place of the heart.*
The more I turned the eye would turn the more,
the more I looked aside the more the eye would seek
the secret land that won my whole regard.

I know that island now as well as I know my head:
its shores are no more to me than my home tides.
I see other hills that I have much desired
become the mere hill-slopes of a known land.
The distant horizons that blazed in the eager mind
shrink to familiar lanes of a quiet shire.

Now I look on these known hills
knowing: this is not home, but away, away
over the green landscapes the heart pursues eternity
and is never satisfied, never filled.
But after all gazing there will come a day
when all landscapes will solace the heart's infinity.

ERNCROGO

The grandson of the winged helmet
who gave this croft its name
burned the blood from his steel
and burnished it in this sour earth
behind a sweating ox.
The centuries have shared him out
among the sullen vanquished:
his eyes, his hair, his stride
adorn the walkers on the moorland path
who pass with peaceful greeting.

A shepherd gazes
over a drystone dyke
leaning upon his crook as on a spear.
Calmly through his blue stare
old Crogo muses on the silent land.

CONVERT

On his way northwards on business from the city
his mind, they say, suddenly became affected
in a way not totally unconnected
with a sneaking spark of unconventional pity
engendered by watching once a steadfast heretic
paying the ultimate price for his trendy views
about life, death, after-death and alleged good news.
The stubborn determination of this fanatic
seems to have been reflected in the watcher's mind
so that he began to shudder and hear voices,
develop a nervous defect of the sight.
Thenceforth from respectability he wholly declined
to a low way of life marked by absurd choices
and soap-box proclamations of seeing the light.

AUTUMN LIGHT

In the slant light of the autumn afternoon
the little waves run gold up to the cladach.
Again it is granted to be here alone
after the dull days, the long dry plodding.

The wind sighing down red and saffron leaves
across the stippled gold and green of the moor.
These sights and sounds I am given should bring all ease,
yet I do not find that which I came here for.

Though distance and peace here are in good supply
for any man of sense who could use them aright
I see but dimly with that inner eye,
must be content with this more worldly light.

RURAL BARD

Who strolls in the rumbling city
courting the urban Muse
must show himself to be witty,
brace up his soul with booze.

Bore on poetical fringes,
his maggot-hole in The Few;
for he knows he won't be printed
till the Big Boys nod him through.

But here in the spuds and pumpkins
may write whatever he will;
the Laureate of the Bumpkins
in Parnassus-under-the-Hill.

Envoi: Squire,
>Country poets are not much read
>though locally well-known;
>even the poacher taps his head
>and points to the poet's home.

HISTORY LESSON

A king, to solve their politics and his,
set rival gangs to fighting on the Inch:
the Cat-men and the Kays. They clanged and battered,
spoiled the axe-edges, locked the Islay hilts.

The Cat-men hired a bandy-legged smith
who lopped the heads off all Clan Kay but one.
He poured his blood into the Tay's cool water
swimming from a Scotland he could not understand
back to an Alba that was still familiar.

It still goes on. Lolling on benches
well railed off from the clans, our rulers watch,
There is no river we can dive into.

A KNELL FOR MR BURNS

I think of you Mr Burns
lying in your death bed;
sweating and sick by turns,
desperate dreams in your head.

In articulo mortis beset
lacking a tailor's fee:
seven guineas in debt
for a worldly vanity.

A day or so after you'd gone
wherever poets go,
the great world looked upon
your fate with affected woe.

Played the Dead March in Saul
behind your silent remains,
having valued hardly at all
the moving heart and brains.

Strange that the living face
should suffer so much rage,
while birth-and-burial place
grew to a pilgrimage.

EXILE

Now all the blood that soaked the heather roots
has dried. The old bards lie forgotten.
Given this new complaisance, these tame towns,
changing my favour I might yet return
to the long strath of flowing memory,
to summer trickle and to winter flood,
contained once more within the loving tribe.

Yet, when all goes, in exile there is honour.
Although I stumble in an alien tongue,
I am not shamed to smothering my own.
These foreign hills may be dressed well enough
to friendlier seeming by the inner eye.

Sometimes a comrade in this banishment
passes a greeting in our old lost speech.
The blood races; the heart lifts up in hope.
Though there is talk between us of returning,
behind the handclasp and the eye's bold eagerness
we know our old ways fail in the far country.

See, from the window, these mountains that top our own,
their valleys riper than our rocky glens.

Why should heart sadden for the native hills?

VIEWPOINT: LAMBDOUGHTY

On the far side of Straiton, on the hill road
the farm names change to Gaelic.
So does the country, bare moorland with no fences,
the rock teeth tearing at the base of clouds.
Look over the covenanting monuments
desperately stabbing the heavens;
you will see beyond the spent volcano of Creag Ealasaid
the distant bounds of the Lordship:
Arran, Kintyre and Jura.

The broken promises of history
are drowned within the silence.

FINDABAR'S SONG

Beside the pool still grows the rowan tree
whose blooded branches shade the monstrous deep;
in all my days of waking day or sleep
he brings a red branch to the shore for me.

No memory of love remains but this:
white skin, black hair, clear eyes and death's dark flood
scarlet of spilling berries and of blood
to me more dear than his forgotten kiss.

TALIESIN: A STRATHCLYDE WINTER

The autumn purple is gone from the hill-slope;
beyond the trees veined on the pale sky,
clouds feather.

Now we have forgotten groves,
abandoned the chase,
like dying men under the raven's eye
we have no cover.

There is no skull in the temple niche,
no blood in the polished cauldron,
no hiss of arrow in the forest trap.
Yet flesh shall not escape mutation.

Our golden torcs exchanged for iron collars,
we reach the apex of a latter day, a course
familiar to the prophets.

A white moon rises
beyond the winter ridge;
between the sight and the thought,
the no-man's-land of the real.

The wind howls in the bloody-handed dawn
chilling the same flesh
the same bone-marrow,
compounded of the same dust,

seeded with the same corruption,
repeated through other eyes
that are the same eyes
as long as the race shall live.

I am Taliesin
I am everyman
where past and future meet.

Trees on the bare ridge, bare veins of their summer selves.
White crown of winter once again
on the eternal mountain.

BEACH WALKING

The ocean's whispered promises,
are worthier of an ear than are most others.
After all journeying and useless striving
I come to walk each evening on the shore.

The sea changes: quicksilver to the world's edge
transmutes to lead before the coming storm.

When first I came here seeking,
a child caught up within eternity,
I knew the hand whose cunning fingers
held the bright sun in place; who with a word
could hold the sea back from its ebb and flow.

On this cold twilight shore
the seabird's cry under the greying night
encourages hope.

The soldier as the bullet speeds towards him
may use the word: *tomorrow*

EXODUS

Aye, we recall the Nile, a wealth of water,
bracelet and breastplate, jewel and chariot,
gold for the gilding of their sweet-spiced dead.
we remember Egypt now, the corn and the oil,
where even a slave could swallow his belly's fill.
What matter the lash, the curse when hunger was stayed?
Warm nights of satiety and sleep.

A wealth of water, and a wealth of wine
that dulled the soul against the passing years.
But here the vision is sharp and the instant bites;
the clear eye seeks the line of a clear horizon.
No mere sobriety has brought this change.

Here, scarcity of food and water stretches
skin over ribs that feel the whip no more;
far better hunger here than burn with weals.
More than the shame of slaves has brought this change.

Here we find only wildness of sand and stone.
Even if one should strike a rock with a staff,
turn it to gold, rather it poured forth water.
More than a thirst in the throat has brought this change.

SECOND WEDDING

Wine, dancing and laughter.
Who should remember the dead?
There would be happiness thereafter.
Stroking his small fair head,
his mother, they said, replaced:
look to the new life to come.
But he stood back, solemn-faced
thinking on his lost one.

FIRST LOVE

Well, that was love, and I remember it,
the hope, the hanging round and the heart's pain,
the coolness, coyness and that off-hand bit
that cut my soul and left me scarcely sane.
Now you are fat and forty and quite plain
I can't imagine what it was I saw
that scented night you passed me in the lane
in that lost sunshine springtime long ago.
Time's fairground mirror to a flatter truth
makes nearer passions by comparing pale;
it's just as well first love does not run smooth
but quits the score with a romantic tale.
I loved you dearly, girl who lived next door;
now, cruel heart, I cannot think what for.

A QUESTION FOR EXPERTS

I do not contest, sirs, that apples fall
at two and thirty feet persec persec
or thereabouts, or that they hit the deck
because of some elusive force you call
gravity; or that mathematics fail
to give to modern warriors a basis
for working out to many decimal places
terminal velocity and the angle of trail.
Only a fool would toy with the suggestion
that E might not quite equal MC squared.
Therefore I took some thought before I dared
raise what I feel you'll think a foolish question:
this fruit that falls at its recorded pace,
what hung it up in its appointed place?

BALLANT

Wha meets ye doun the shaw, my suin
while I bide here ma lane,
the simmer's gloamin nearlie duin,
aside a bare herthstane?
Whit limmer bides yir cumin,
thro the shedda daurk an warm?
I fear sae dern a wumman
maun shairlie bring ye herm.

Doun the shaw: *down in the wood* ma lane: *on my own* limmer: *hussy* sheddas: *shadows* dern: *secret*

There's nane that huuds me nou mither
ablo the whuspran trees,
nae soun but the souchin brainch mither
that steers in the forenicht breeze;
nocht but a wae-wan face I see
aside the river's brink;
it gliffs up frae the deep et me
whan I kneel doun tae drink.

FORCED MARCH

Late one evening on the long road
between one camp and yet another,
he passed a village where the torches glowed
and sparks flew upwards in the still weather.

To droning reeds and the tap of drums
a swaying girl danced among the flames;
the jingling gold on her weaving arms
threw him a share of the random gleams.

Embers of days he had thought long dead
kindled once more to remembered pain
for the round arms and the golden head
in a land that he would not see again.

---

whuspran: *whispering* souchan: *sighing* brainch: *branch* nocht: *nothing* wae-wan: *white with grief* lochan: *small lake* gliffs: *glances*

DRINKS

Early, there are the pleasures of the senses;
later remain the pleasures of the mind,
which in their turn, have certain recompenses.
Like cider-pips-and-all before good wine.

Now, even though my palate's more discerning
my youthful taste's not quite beneath the pall;
I sip my clear thin wine to drown a yearning
for the old cloudy scrumpy, pips and all.

LISTED HOUSE: STEWARTRY

After the laird had built him this grand house
stepping foul by the ford the heir was drowned,
in the small hours after a night's carouse;
a month went by before the corpse was found.

The old mansion wears its three hundred years;
preserved windows look on the tidy lawn;
down by the riverside a grey mist clears,
trees weep for old shades against the dawn.

Walking early beneath the first bird song,
feel how the morning fills with summer joy;
look down to the ford where a step went wrong,
where weeds tangled the throat of the singing boy.

NURSEMAIDS AND SOLDIERS

The Duke of Dedleigh's Horse Hussars
wore jackets bright with lace and spangles.
In twilight swaggerings through the park
you'd hear their spurs and medals jangle.

The nursemaids eyed them with delight;
they swooned and dropped with admiration,
arranged that their off-duty nights
should co-incide for assignation.

But sabres sliced the handsome skulls;
guns blew strong legs off at the thighs,
while master craftsmen, rich but dull
enjoyed the nursemaids' midnight sighs.

Bright trumpets ringing in the head,
the fancy coat, the prancing steed
recruit replacements for the dead.
A sober stock maintains the breed.

LOCHAR WATTER

Heich biggin an heich maitter
warld's misure o walth's fee
in the lang wuid by the Lochar Watter
yon's whaur I wad raither be.

---

heich: *high*

Bricht siller and gowden pletter
the purpie claith an the cramosie,
in the lang wuid by the Lochar Watter
yon's whaur I wad raither be.

Prood palace and lear's letter,
faur citie and fremit sea,
in the lang wuid by the Lochar Watter
yon's whaur I wad raither be.

The wearie years dinna bield better
frae auld myndans that winna dee,
in the lang wuid by the Lochar Watter,
the ae place that I canna be.

---

cramosie: *crimson* lear: *learning* fremit: *foreign* bield: *protect* myndans: *memories*

BLOSSOM, BERRY, FALL

BY THE RIVER

From the Black Loch to the Glen of Rushes
I walk silent in the shade of trees
on leaf-mould paths where the clawing bushes
reach out to hinder the one who strays.

The quiet swan and his white lover
breast on calm water their ripples down.
By the dark brink of the still river
there are no footprints beside my own.

The season passes: blossom, berry, fall
thicken the carpet beneath my feet;
like a swift bird through the festive hall
swoops the year on through the fading light.

GULL

Being set to court the wise men and the wits
I took up early with the city's ways,
spending in drink and chatter all my days,
to follow all their foolishness and fits,
aping the latest fancy and the phrase
from the wag's tongue and what high fashion says
and thus I split my poor soul into bits.

But being wakened from this idle dream
I went to walk on my own fathers' land,
half way between the fertile and the sand,
watching the dawn and the blue night's moonbeam,
machair and reed and rock on every hand,
far from the city tavern's prattling band,
hearing on bleak shores only the gull's high scream.

WINTER

This dayset, from the north a keen wind sighs
sorrow for winter on its bitter cold,
leaving a sunshine gift of beaten gold
that on the moorland in great glory lies,

before long darkness comes in the year's dying.
Men will hide fear under the high feast
that brings the new light rising from the waste
for seed to liven where the snow is lying.

For all spring sowing and the summer striving,
all wordy prayer in righteousness or sin,
dead winter comes with snow to shroud us in,
the word of the cold wind for a last shriving.

CAT ACCIDENT

A small sad tiger, sent to sleep too young.
Behind the apple tree, just two feet deep
the ground was hard, a flintstone to my steel.
I curled his body in a last cat-sleep.

In his brown bed of earth he seemed content.
I wished him well, wherever he had gone:
into cat-nothingness or transmigration.
Hope I look half as good when I am done.

ON CARRICK GROUND

My eyes have sight that comes from other eyes
that looked on Arran through the centuries;
on Ailsa Craig, Creag Ealasaidh, Carraig Alasdair,
the rocky throne where mad king Suibhne sat
half way between Dal Araidh and Dal Riada;
Lailocen country, ancient home of bards:
Bluchbard and Cian, Taliesin, Burns,
The Hielant Captain and Mac Iain Deors'.

I go along drove roads past the old steadings
graced with their Celtic names now long forgotten
by ignorant generations; cottages with names
changed by the fugitives from southern cities
to pretty hollyhock-names that hide the craigs,
rolling un-Saxon moorland, hostile ghosts
whose voices rustle in insulated lofts.

Earning their frugal bread with spade and mattock
my kin have seen these hills for centuries,
sharing the same soil with the lairds and kings.
For all their dwelling under the rude thatch
these are the folk on whom I look with pride:
men of my name who neighboured Robert Burns,
who dug like Eoghan in the Celtic soil,
making sweet songs enough upon sour ground.

Why should it matter anything to me,
a desert moorland and its pauper soil,
beyond the merest chance of ancestry?
How does the bound and wounded soul of Scotland
stand against learned Athens, noble Florence?
These rounded Carrick hills, these craigy muirs,
Arran's high Comb, the long reach of Kintyre,
the names that mark the land with a lost Gaelic,
why should these take such primacy of place,
loom without reason in a travelled vision?
Yet as the bird and salmon seek their ground
so does the foot walk best on native soil,
the spirit find on the bare hills of home
more warmth than glows on fertile alien fields.

So, from the humble seed that fleshed my bones
I build a pride as high as any prince;
better this clean descent from common folk,
who lived upon this ground in bitter toil,
whose eyes, as mine, looked upon Carrick land
by the long firth in all its changing seasons.

The deed to their estate is my own marrow;
our eyes look to the bounds of a shared horizon.

HIGH ON DRUMCONNARD

I

High on Drumconnard the eye is drawn to the sea,
to the Lordly Isles that lie on the rim of the West,
but further and nearer than they the call and the quest
that will neither come at my bidding nor let me be.

Far from Drumconnard the vision and yet near,
far from the mountain peak and the sloping land;
for all that the silence whispers on every hand,
long am I lost though yon far horizon is clear.

II

Drumconnard Cottage stands firm on the moor
like a laird's castle from its vantage here;
the windows open when the day is clear
on a wide slew that rolls down from its door.

A king would take Drumconnard did he know
of that long flowing in a peasant eye,
a green domain, alone and far on high,
where the wild walkers and black cattle go.

LADY RECLUSE

In the long gloom of that tall mansion there,
lives an old, tired and miserable dame,
cynosure once of many a grand affair
become a mere dog's tail of little fame
but for the faded blazon of a name.
Her footsteps ring unheard along the hall,
for she's stone-deaf and no one comes to call.

Under the weeds beside the wrought-iron gates
the weekly goods are left at the drive end.
Beside the empty stable no groom waits,
no wheels crush gravel by the carriage bend.
The postman swears no kinsmen ever send
a formal season's card or birthday wishes
to lie among dull silver and crazed dishes.

Lifting provision by the empty lodge
the locals say 's the only time she'll bow.
whatever fabric autumn gales dislodge,
she will not ask for one to come and do.
Goodwill might visit, but from trial know
she'll send them packing with a mumbled curse
as if they'd come intent to steal her purse.

The children come to play their haunted games,
assuming safety from the cloistered witch,
who, even if she heard their folklore names
is prisoned by the intervening ditch.
Some day a messenger will come to fetch
what's left of her patrician flesh and bone,
and carve a lozenge on the meagre stone.

ARE YOU THERE, MR PUNCH?

Down on the beach, the Punch and Judy show
contained within its horrid, scary plot
a simple foretaste of the human lot.
The red-nosed tyrant of the squeaky crow
gave us male-chauvinist-piggery blow by blow;
killed hangman, death's head, devil, on the trot;
like all true rogues, for all his sins, uncaught.
We pondered, naughty children down below.

Oh, crafty Punchinello, nose and chin
touching each other, velvet suit and bells;
our dreams were haunted by your wicked smile.

How could we know the world we'd venture in
more frightful yet, for all your gleeful yells,
than skeleton, policeman, hangman, crocodile.

CELTIC LEGEND

Up here by Loch Roghainn
flies dance on still water,
in quiet summer gloaming
and none other roaming
but bonnie black horses.

Not me who'd be idle
to gallop till morning,
had I but a bridle
with stirrup and saddle
and silver adorning.

No rich-mounted harness
in hand or in stable.
the elders have torn us
from witch-hags who warn us
with old, lying fables.

STILLNESS

A whisper in the calm of the red evening:
stir now, old ghost, to haunt me as you did.
There is no answer to the hopeful calling
but a new stillness in the heart and head.

The fenceposts stand like soldiers in the ranks;
campion and foxglove in the summer hedge.
The stream lies low and calm below its banks,
the wild herd gone now from the forest edge.

CELTIC CHAPEL

A rusted grating in the ancient wall:
in those cold squares the child would frame his face.
The roofless gables held their light and space
where monks came singing to the vesper call.

This, they said, used to be the home of God,
the fading whisper of an ancient tale.
A silent chantry without altar rail,
bare ruin reaching for the sailing cloud.

TRACING YOUR ANCESTORS

Who knows, you might turn up a duke
or the mouldering horror of a famous monster;
you can always boast of the toffs and forget the rogues.

Among my own lot I found neither dukes nor crooks.
Horse-copers, ploughmen, tinkers, hewers of wood,
drawers of beer and soldiers of private rank.

Ah well, I said, common douce folk enough
who never started a war or passed a tyrannical law
or ground the faces of poor men in the dust.

Sour grapes, said Burke and Debrett.
If your vulgar genes had been shoved over a bit
you'd be as big a bully and snob as the rest.

OAKWOOD AND GALL

The tall trees sway over Drumnakillie
three lifespans long for each trunk of oak;
the berried rowan and the jagged holly
stretch a long mile on the hillside's back.

Shenachan's* company no longer meet there
in the high *doire* of the poet band;
each twig that cracks underneath your feet there,
marks out the circle of the druid ground.

Bluchbard and Cian of the Northern Gentry
and great Aneirin† gather there no more;
the high bold singers have all left the country;
black silence reigning where was joy before.

Smooth city tongues discard the native birthright
to lisp bad verses into duller ears;
they smothered noonday with their Celtic Twilight. . . .
the devil choke them on their Saxon sneers.

---

doire: *an oak wood* (pr. durra (Gaelic))

* Shenachan (v. Cliar Sheanachain) was the leader of a Gaelic 'poet band'.
† Bluchbard, Aneirin and Cian were poets of the 'Bretts' of south-west Scotland, otherwise known as the Gwyr y Gogledd (The Northern Men).

HERO'S CHILD 1927

Watching stiff ranks beside a granite cross
he heard a bugle sound for distant men;
looked up at faces that were grim with loss
for the old crowd who would not come again.

Sad formal words on the chill morning air
masked a sharp truth from innocence alone:
how far the still town was from that affair
of screams and bloody flesh, and steel-ruined bone.

INSHORE GALE

With too much canvas the tall birches sail
across the roaring land against the cloud.
The wood runs free before the autumn gale.

Soon frosty doldrums will becalm each tree,
as deep in silence as the gale was loud;
bare masts and yards locked in an icy sea.

NIGHT CALLER

The starkest is the earliest memory.
A dark newcomer in the quiet room.
Now it is time, she is to come with me;
I am sent to take her to another home.

Child vision mingles the dream and real.
Phantom or fact, the adult mind is clear:
the low sure voice; the woman's body still,
the child upright, tearful and without fear.

ROWANS

Near freedom's end the rowan berries came
like blood splashed on the posts of autumn's door.
We made guns of wheeled weeds and blew red bullets
that squashed to discs between the barn and byre.
For all the laughing and running and yelling and hiding
there was a grip at the heart as the sweet days ended.
School in a week, and yet another year,
a new adventure, growth and a kind of learning.

Now freedom's all that's left and the berries come
scarlet on fading green in the long wood.
I feel the grip at the heart for the summer's ending.
Gone are the cowboy-and-indian peashooter days,
but I stand in the still hour on winter's threshold
hoping still for growth and a kind of learning.

MAKING TRACKS

MARKED PASSAGE

I happened on a verse you underlined
in the small book you loved so long ago;
unseen before, I knew then how you pined
and lost your life's young brightness under woe.

Saw then the reason for that sought oblivion:
a flight from circumstance's narrow way.
Remembered distance and the silent tongue
that should have spoken in your troubled day.

SEALLTAINN THAR CHLUAIDH

Cuimhne leam oidhche dhorcha ghailleanach,
deireadh na Semhna, stoirm a' togail sgleat,
gaoth mhòr bheucach, bhagrach
'na deann-ruith seachad air Arainn is cathair Shuibhne
is mi air tràigh eadar m'athair 's mo sheanair,
is greim teann aca air gach làmh agam.
Ged nach b'urrainn dhaibh m' aodann a dhìonadh
bho sgiùrsair guineach nam frasan,
le acair daingeann gach taobh dhiom
cha b'urrainn don duile mo bhriseadh.

Sin thanaig onfhaidhean eile orm
bho aigeann dhorcha gun ghrunnd
is mi gu lèir gun acair,
le làmh neo-chinnteach air an stiùir.

Ach fhuair mi aig a cheann thall
sàbhailte gu cala, agus tha fèath ann.

Linne Chluaidh mar sgàthan, ciùin fom shùil.

LOOKING OVER CLYDE

I remember a dark night of gales
at the end of November, a storm lifting the slates
a great roaring, threatening wind in its mad dash past Arann and
Suibhne's chair (Ailsa Craig)
when I was on the shore between my father and grandfather
who had a tight grip on both my hands
although they could not keep the stinging whip of the showers from
my face
with a strong anchor on both sides of me
the elements could not break me.

Then other tempests came upon me
from a dark bottomless abyss
and I was completely without an anchor
an uncertain hand on the tiller.

But in the end I arrived
safely to harbour, and there is a calm.

Firth of Clyde like a mirror, gentle under my eyes.

YONNER AWA

Yonner awa, faur owre Clauchrie Tap
the smirrin clouds o the gloamin fa
in murnin reebans doun in ilka glack
tae thowe the shairds o the winter snaw.
Ma thochts are gruppit wi a skeer mindin
o a biggin faur owre the muir awa . .
the brawest airt o ma halflin bydin
whaur ma hert raise up wi the daylicht's daw.

The Makkars say whit the hert lacks
is skailt abreid in the licht o Mey . .
the morn it micht be that the suin braks
tae pent the hulls wi the wairtid's blae;
but thare's nae saw for whit canna hale . .
a grienin eftir a santit day.
Thare's nae licht in onie lift kin steal
the lang ladin o a lastie wae.

---

smirrin: *drizzling* murnin reebans: *mourning ribbons* glack: *cleft* shairds: *shards*
gruppit: *held* skeer: *clear* mindin: *memory* biggin: *building* airt: *place* halflin: *stripling* daw: *dawn* Makkars: *Poets* skailt abreid: *scattered away* wairtid: *time of change (weather)* saw: *salve* hale: *heal* greinin: *longing* santit: *blessed* lift: *sky* ladin: *load* lastie wae: *enduring sorrow*

SUNDAY SCHOOL

Our Mr Sanctus said the money went
to educate the heathen; while we sat
too young to take the adult sacrament,
but learning all the holy words off pat.

With the good ladies in the sacred Hall
we touched on tales we scarcely understood,
vague sins that made no sense to us at all,
although Miss Prism seemed to think them rude.

I watched the dancing motes of shining dust,
dreamt of the heathen lying in the sun,
and how my offered penny surely must
make plain to him how Three is always One.

Woke to unyielding benches and the smell
of fading naphthalene on Sunday cloth
and thought how naked heathens, bound for hell,
required no salve from the Corrupting Moth.

COCKTAILS FROM SHAKESPEARE

King Duncan's bedroom splashed about with gore
resulted in gate-crashing apparitions.
Lay plastic sheets upon the bedroom floor
and marry wisely, if you have ambitions.

Thinking that he was cuckold to a hanky
the Moor doused lights and strangled his career.
If you suspect your wife of hanky-panky
prudential ignorance may come less dear.

If on some hazy evening you should fall
for a mere Bottom with a donkey's head,
next morning make staunch efforts to recall
exactly what it was you did . . . and said.

Don't make a date for Troilus to meet Cressid
(which seems a kindness, seen in isolation)
a union that turns out to be unblessed
may do no favours to your reputation.

When at long last you know you've got it made
though sure the boss's chair will last your time,
don't wait like Julius for the dagger-blade
before composing a good exit-line.

If driven to barbiturates and booze,
the bodkin's present-day equivalent,
read up the Prince's speech before you choose.
The method makes no odds to where you're sent.

When mixing with the smart set's biggest spenders
those argosies may fail to come to port:
your meat and blood are safe from money-lenders
but plastic cards may get you into court.

However macho you may think you are
the servile wifeling has become bad news.
Better to meet a girl-friend in the bar
for dining dutch, than take to taming shrews.

A FAUR CRY FRAE AUCHINLECK

Tae be a Scot yung Jamie Bos'll thocht
a wee thing waur nor yon auld het affliction
that smit him later frae a warm addiction
tae leddies coortit whan in drink, or bocht.
In London toun nae maitter hou he wrocht
he fund that Scotchness wes a sair constriction,
sae twustit aw his mainners an his diction
tae get Auld Sammie's saicrets in his aucht.

The Doctor's Messan set a Scottish paitren
tae mak oor hoggs thair Scottish lugmairks tine.
For speakin Scots wee duddie bairns are skelpit.

An nou in sudron twangs ye'll hear thaim rettlin . .
the heirs of Jamie Bos'll's social line,
wha say: *I'm Scottish but I cannot help it.*

FITSIDES WI A PROOD HIZZIE

(Horace 1.25)

The dure that swung wi guidwull on its hinges
is no sae thrang the day as it wes then,
whan ilka callant rettled on yer wunnock
wi chuckie stanes tae gar ye cry thaim ben.

---

het: *hot* smit: *infected* wrocht: *worked* in his aucht: *into his possession* hoggs: *sheep*
lugmairks: *earmarks* tine: *lose* duddie bairns: *scruffy children* skelpit: *smacked*
sudron twangs: *southern accents (English)*

thrang: *busy* callant: *youth*

D'ye mind hou yince thay tirlit on yer door-sneck
the guid auld days whan ye'd hear the halflin cry:
Haw Libbie, hinnie, wad ye hae me stivven
while ye ligg sleepin on yer ain inbye?

Ye'll shuin be lichtlied by thir hornie laudies:
ye'll greet yir lane doun a tuim an clartie close,
the wund o a mirk nicht skreichin frae the hielants ..
nae mune tae licht yer chaumer, cauld an bose.

Juist lik an auld mear mindan on the couser
freitin an keistie, liggin on yir ain. . . .
yir breist will lowe wi the stangs o luve rejeckit
an nae braw jo near haund tae smoor the pain,

Syne ken the callants wad raither the green ivy,
or the braw leaves growin daurk on the myrtle shaw;
auld crynit brainches they gie tae the wund's pleisure,
grey winter's gemm, an watch thaim flee awa.

GALLOWA SPRING

The gowd is back upon the brae
Millyea has tint the snaw;
lown is the northart sough the day
an warm the wastlin blaw.

---

lichtlied: *treated with contempt* tuim: *empty* boss: *hollow* couser: *travelling stallion*
keistie: *randy* crynit: *withered*

Blythe nou wha tholed the wintertide
its crannreuch cauld an lang.
Green, green the shaws on braw Kenside
an sweet the laverock's sang.

THE LONELY PLACE

This is the gentle land of the white swan,
the lonely resting-place of journeying geese,
where graceful woodland borders the river-lawns
and the cracking twig startles the shy deer.

This is the valley where winter gales go
roaring through the dark ranks of bare trees;
where on summer evenings the long twilights glow
under the breeze that rustles the crowning leaves.

These are the hills where the long shadows lie
where the quiet birds upon calm waters rest,
where the green country stretches under the eye
and joy kindles again in the troubled breast.

ON LOCH KEN SIDE

This day the lest snaw liggs atour Millyea,
skyre lift in Mairch hansels the springtime in
as yince in bairntid owre the western sea
the sicht o Arran's kaim ablo the suin,
tynin the croun o glentin majestie
gied a blythe warrantie o spring begun.
I hae growne frae the fair heid tae the lyart pow,
but the yae hert sings this day wi the yae lowe.

Up frae the rashes, heich abune the trees,
intil the lift wi eldritch skraich an cletter,
in thair ticht squadrons tovin, the wild geese
I watch in joy wing frae the braid lown watter.
Tho een behaud, it is the saul that sees
mair in the motion nor cauld ee-sicht's maitter.
This I hae lang kent, but I canna mak
frae the hert's kennin, whit plain mense will tak.

JUVENILIA AMORIS

Young, I wrote love-songs, heartfelt but not good,
of moon and June and love and mist and stars
on backs of envelopes in gloomy bars;
like betting slips. *they'd* not have understood:
the verse that *they* preferred was short and crude
on curious sexual antics and class wars . .
the coarse accompaniment of frothing jars.
Limericks they liked, provided they were rude.

Such gems I hid away in private places
until I worked up courage to donate
lines to the latest love. Alas, alack . .

from early loves I had but slight embraces.
Do they read now with laughter, love or hate?
I sweat to think about them, looking back

TROMLAIGHE

Nuair a thuit tùr-taighean àrda Bailtean a' Chomhnaird
an dèidh na crìonachadh bha air na daoine
le tinneas, bochdainn, galar spioradail,
sgaoil am fuigheal as gach larach luidegach.
Bha cothrom na Fèinne aig an Fheadhainn Mòra
a dh'fhàs cho beartach an Baile-Mhamon-Eucorach,
gunnachan is geamairean a thoirt
gu frìthean fasail leudaichte ùra.
An dràsd 's a rithist gheibhear truaghan
an impis marbhadh le goirt, ag èaladh
mar choineanach tre raineach,
is cò an duine a choireachadh a charaid
is e 'cuir stad air leithid sin de dhòrainn
le urchair bhaidheil 's e gu tur gun mhi-rùn.

Air neo. . . .

Dh'fhàs an Fheadhain Mora reamhar 's cadalach
le sògh is geòcaireachd is somaltachd,
daorach air ceannard fhreiceadan gach oidhche
ag creidsinn gu robh na treubhan borba samhach.
Dh'èirich luchd-cagarsaich nan sràidean suarach,
a' toirt gach inneal a bu dlùithe dhan làimh,
buideal-theine, beiglid, sgian is speal.
Builgeanan fuileach sna Jacuzzis *ac'*
is teas 's na saunas *nach do dh'iarr iad.*
Thog na tràillean a'Mhaighdean
an Roinn Malairt nan Stoc.
Chìteadh na cinn 'gan ròladh,
fo shùilean dalla chomputair,
   s an sgìamhach amaideach samhach.

NIGHTMARE

When the high tower-blocks fell in the Cities of the Plain
after the withering that came on the people
with disease, poverty, spiritual sickness,
the remainder scattered from each shabby ruin.
There was every chance for the great ones
who grew so rich in Unjust-Mammon-City
to take their gamekeepers
to the empty and extended new grouse-moors.
Now and again a wretch would be found
on the point of starving with hunger, crawling
like a rabbit through bracken,
and who would blame his friend
for putting an end to that kind of misery
with a good-natured shot entirely without malice.

or else. . . .

The Great Ones grew fat and sleepy
with luxury, gluttony and sloth,
the captain of the guard drunk every night
believing the wild tribes to be at peace.
The whisperers arose in the mean streets,
lifting every tool that was close to hand,
petrol-bomb, bayonet, knife and scythe.
Bloody bubbles in their jacuzzis
and a heat in the saunas that they had not sought.
The slaves raised up the guillotine
in the Stock Market building.
Heads were seen rolling
under the blind eyes of computers,
and their foolish squeaking was silenced.

Chuala mi mac-talla, nam dhùisg le clisgeadh eagalach:

*'Chan eil aingidheachd dhaoine air a cumail fo smachd
le feansaichean meirgeach Bhelsen'.*

I heard an echo, waking in a start of fear:

'The cruelty of men is not imprisoned
within the rusty fences of Belsen.'

OBITUARY FOR CAPTAIN TAIKLE

From brassbounder to captain, all those years,
of storm and tempest, Doldrums still and blue;
he would not reef to cover up his fears,
tough as the teak his youthful timbers grew.

Barely fifteen and hanging out on yards,
hand for the ship, another for himself,
sails trim and square as any pack of cards,
running and beating stowed his hold with wealth.

Grog-ballasted he swaggered through the port;
he cursed and swore at lubber shipping-clerks;
it wasn't drink or temper breached the fort,
or living over-well on skipper's perks . .

but little deadly South American darts . .
so small they can't be seen without a glass,
that set their hooks in bones and brains and hearts,
and bring strong men to many a sorry pass.

Poor Captain Taikle glowered from his chair
till he could hardly move; no girls, no drink;
no hands of nap in Futtock's Tavern there . .
since at the end he couldn't even think.

Tough as a turk's head, never known to bend,
bolder than brass and better than me or you;
a square-rig seadog scuttled in the end
with tiny darts, by a lady in Peru.

THREE WOMEN

They say that man was much disturbed by love,
though some would say, more by the lack of it;
a crying infant in a midnight bed,
a dying woman at the back of it.

He took to strong drink in the middle days
to crush the memories of the sober mind,
until the woman that he took to wife
fled from the shadows that he hid behind.

The last kind lover of the autumn day,
before the night cooled to the grip of frost,
set clearer vision in a calmer eye
of long years wasted to the new love's cost.

POET'S WALK 1796

Exciseman Burns wannert the kittle toun,
his wame aw wersh wi drink, his hert wi gaw;
wha tentit him in this thrawn bit ava?
Nou nocht tae dae but staucher roun an roun
frae White Sands tae Midsteeple, up and doun
the banks o Nith, aye waitin for the caa
o the Caledonian Muse. The bitch had fled awa
an widna yield a sang tae a gauger's tune.

Thro grey Dumfries the cauld broun watter gaed,
droonin the speirit as it smoort the rime
oot tae a stick's tap on the causey stanes.

Whiles the faur city flittert in his heid.
As daurk St Michael's bydit for his time
the smirr o Solway stoundit in his banes.

---

wannert: *wandered* kittle: *wicked* wame: *stomach* wersh: *sour* gaw: *gall* tentit: *heeded* thrawn: *stubborn, perverse* nocht: *nothing* staucher: *stagger* gauger: *exciseman* smoort: *smothered* causey: *pavement* flittert: *fluttered* smirr: *a penetrating misty rain* stoundit: *ached*

AIK TREE

Yestreen the gale wes rettlin gless an sclait.
I heard a muckle dunt in the mirk nicht;
an oorie thing, I waukent in a fricht
gruppit, I thocht, atween the shears o fate.
It wesna Clotho makkin a lest date
as I could plainlie see in the morn's licht.
Yon muckle aik that stuid sae strang an ticht
bi yon byornar Januar blest wes bait.

I hae kent men lik aiks, hae felt the dunt
made on the human speerit whan thay fell
whaur fuit micht tramp on tapmaist brainch an ruit.

Whiles bi sic trunks ye'll see a birkie strunt
an brag as if he'd brocht it doun himsel,
but daurna kick, for fear he'll stave his fuit.

HIELANT JOHN 1930

He mairched aboot the gitters o ma bairnheid
three medals on his breist an the pipes soundin
faur, faur frae Wipers an the bluidy Somme
in this laund fit for heroes tae stairve in.

Yestreen: *last night* sclait: *slate* muckle dunt: *great thump* mirk: *black* oorie: *eerie* gruppit: *gripped* aik: *oak* byornar: *extraordinary* bait: *beaten* birkie: *a conceited person*

gitters: *gutters* bairnheid: *childhood*

I couldna pass him on a Setterday,
athoot gien up ma hard-wan penny;
ye're daft, said ma auld-mither,
he'll spenn it on the drink.
But I couldna jist gae bye him.

Yince, pipes ablo his oxter
he heard the rettle
o my aums in his tinnie.

He cried oot eftir me
ither an aith or a blissin.
Ma tackets duntit the causey as I ran
awa. awa frae a kennawhat in his een.

LUCRETIUS, BUIK THREE SNEDDIT

He aye threips oan that when ye're deid ye're deid.
Thae's be nae girning in ablo the mool ..
nor tholin Clootie's salutorie dool.
Thir heuks an whups an flames aboot yir heid
or haloes, gin ye jouk yon sair remede,
are products o the joukerie-poukerie schuil ...
sae daith bed prayers, the cauld repentance stuil
een masses fur yir saul wull dae nae guid.

---

auld-mither: *grandmother* yince: *once* oxter: *armpit* aums: *alms* tinnie: *tin cup*
ither: *either* aith: *oath* causey: *pavement* kennawhat: *something indescribable* een: *eyes*

threips: *insists* girnin: *complaining* mool: *earth, clay* tholin: *enduring* dool: *distress*
heuks: *hooks* jouk: *duck* sair: *sore* remede: *cure* joukerie-poukery: *jiggery-pokery*

Think deep on the dern power o usquebae. . . .
the staucherin limb, the menseless bletherin tung . . .
yeskin an soomin een an howff-yaird fecht.

Ye see what jist a wee drap drink kin dae
tae skaith the strang yauld spierit o the yung?
Mair mauchtie dunts come frae yon daurker dracht.

SOLDIER'S RETURN

After they took away the plaster cast
he went to convalesce in Belle Falaise.
He wrote such lovely letters from the place
before he came to stay with us at last.

I've never seen a house so tall and grand.
When the sun shines upon its diamond panes
they flash and glisten all across the land
as if the castle burned with crystal flame.
Beside the pillars of the great front door
are two bronze beasts: I do not know their name,
but wonderful the hall they stand before.
Ivory tables in tall rooms are kept;
brocaded seats broidered with coats-of-arms;
the bed wherein a king and mistress slept
when free to bed for her erotic charms
after the royal succession was assured.
I've put some weight on and they say I'm cured.

---

dern: *secret* usquebae (uisge beatha): *whisky* staucherin: *staggering* menseless: *stupid* yeskin: *hiccup* soomin: *swimming* howff-yaird: *inn-yard* skaith: *injure* yauld: *sturdy* mauchtie dunts: *heavy blows* dracht (ch as in 'loch'): *draught*

His pension money hardly pays our keep.
When he got home, his leg broke out again;
there's not much nourishment in bread and scrape.
Without the pills he curses with the pain.

SOLSTICE

Trees, still as reflection
in the forest's oratory.

Sidesmen to these aisles,
sycamore, rowan, beech
the needled conifer.

See, the bare branches
bones for spring's resurrection.

AGHAIDH RI H-AGHAIDH

Mar bhalach a rithisd air bruach na h-aibhne,
lùb mi ghlùn a dh'fhaicinn a nuas 'san doimhneachd.
Cha robh breac, no geadas, no doirbeag tighinn nam lèirsinn,
ach a mhàin sgàthan dubh, doilleir, fèathach,
is bodach liath teagmhach,
a' sealltainn orm gu cròsda.
Bha mi gun fhoighidinn gun do chuir e bacadh
air aodann na b'òige choimhead suas orm
los gun innseadh e ciamar a bha
leithid de dh'aighear 's mi òg,
is iasg leisg fodham air la briagha samhraidh.

FACE TO FACE

Like a boy again on the river-bank
I knelt down to see into the depths.
There was no trout or pike, or minnow in my vision
only a black mirror, opaque, calm
and a suspicious greybeard looking irritably up at me.
I was impatient at his preventing a younger face from gazing up to me
that would tell me how I felt such joy when young
and a lazy fish below me on a beautiful summer's day.

CLARSAIR

Ri pongan finealta fonnmhor nan cruit gleusda
is bodhar na suinn an diugh 'san t-seòmar àrd;
is feàrr leò geòcaireachd seach amhran bhàrd.
Do chraobh bhriagh nan teud cha toir iad èisdeachd.

Is liath mo cheann is chan iarrainn a nis ach ceòl,
coma leam gach call eile ma mhaireas sin;
'nam aonar a' cluinntinn fuaim na clàrsaich binn
'san talla a bhoillsgeas le airgead is òr.

HARPER

To the delicate harmony of the tuned lyre
the heroes are deaf today in the high room;
they prefer gluttony to the songs of poets.
To the beautiful tree of harps they give no ear.

My head is white and I seek nothing now but music,
I care nothing for the loss of all else if that will endure;
alone and listening to the sweet harp's sound
in the hall that shines with silver and gold.

SPINNLE AN LEEM

Doun, doun, the warld gaes doun
the michtie biggins fa
the castle's aislars skailt aroun,
mak fit-stuils for the craw,
the cowpit rucks o banes will shuin
be sawn amang thaim aa.

The birlin yird is nae man's mull
for aw thay howp an ken
tae wab on leems o guid or ill
the braidclaith weird o men;
tae cleik an cross thair skeerie wull
the yairn is wund again.

---

michtie biggins: *great buildings* aislars: *ashlars* skailt: *scattered:* cowpit: *tumbled* rucks: *ricks* sawn: *sown* birlin: *spinning* yird: *earth* mull: *mill* howp an ken: *hope and know* wab: *weave* leems: *looms* weird: *fate* cleik and cross: *figures in a dance* skeerie: *flighty* yairn: *yarn* wund: *wound*

LAST RACE

Broken on a wheel
a hare rests by the road verge,
shrouded by his guts,
his strong hind legs still striving
to beat that sly tortoise, death.

LANG I BIDE EFTIR THE LAVE*

Lang I bide eftir the lave.
A shaird o the auld warld tae me
that wes langsyne sae mirrie an brave,
is this warld athoot yon companie.

Nou thir auld singers are gane
til an airt whaur nae makkar is thrang,
faur ben in a lown o ma ain,
I dwyne for the want o a sang.

Yae sang in the leid o the laund
that wes langsyne sae mirrie an brave,
frae a tung o yon braw makkar baund.
Lang, lang I bide eftir the lave.

---

* From the Gaelic of Duncan MacRyrie c. 1630

the lave: *the rest* airt: *place* thrang: *busy* faur ben: *deep within* lown: *calm* dwyne: *wither* leid: *language*

THE CHOICE

'Sae I micht lieve on yird,
as hire-man tae anither,
better be this than laird
owre aw the deid thegither.'
    Homer *Od.*XI *489–91*

Eftir yon wearie daurg frae burn tae heidrigg
cowpin the furrs owre in the droukin rain,
A tane ma smoke abune the bothie kist
an kent ye wadna sett on there again.

Auld Meg went corp-white whan the postie cam . .
her guidman deid in France owre twintie year,
an nou yirsel; but she's a gash yin thon,
wi runkilt chafts that cudna shaw a tear.

Gin ye'd steyed fermin an no wan awa,
(syne ithers sodgert, ye wad sodger tae)
tho cowpin furrs is nae gret life ava,
ye'd hae yir smoke upo this kist the day.

---

lieve: *live* yird: *earth* daurg: *days work* burn: *stream* heidrigg: *field's edge* cowpin: *turning over* furrs: *furrows* droukin: *soaking* bothie kist: *chest in servant's room* sett: *sit* guidman: *husband* gash: *grim* runkilt chafts: *wrinkled cheeks* syne: *since* sodgert: *soldiered*

A PUSHION PEN PISTLE

Ye've no been bidden tae The Carse, Rab Burns
syne yon nicht Captain Riddel flung ye oot...
ongauns ye say ye canna mind aboot,
tho we ken ye were fou an tint the hairns.
Eftir the Sabines hud thair Roman bairns
thay got on weel eneuch withooten doot;
no lik yirsel, ye muckle drucken bruit
tae grup a leddie in yir coorse-lik airms.

I kent thay wad begowk ye in the end
for aw yir gesterin aboot the toun
tae mak daft lauds an glaikit lassies geck.

Ye grew that prood yir rigbane wadna bend.
Yon Mistress Riddel's fairlie dingt ye doun
for steckin up yir heid abune the feck.

---

pushion: *poison* pistle: *letter* syne: *since* ongauns: *'goings on'* tint: *lost* hairns: *brains*
bairns: *children* muckle: *big* begowk: *make a fool of* gesterin: *grandiose swaggering*
glaikit: *silly* geck: *stare* rigbane: *backbone* dingt: *knocked* the feck: *the mob*

WILD HAIRST

Warm in the sark-sleeves o an autumn day,
I rypit busses o black berries, played
an hour or twa the hunt-and-gaither trade
o oor first auncestors. Thay didna pey
siller for yon hairst fruicts binna the wey
o human sweit for ilka mait they laid
on the cave flair; but I hae heard it said
fear o the unkent drave thair thochts agley.

You muckle bounlessness in winter's daurk,
the ooriness that dwalt in ilka tree,
the lang tuim howes, cauld in the souchin wund.

I gaithert berries whaur the brammles mark
the faurmaist mairches o the lave that's free,
feart for aw human daurkness, fell an blinn.

---

hairst: *harvest* sark: *shirt* rypit: *plundered* siller: *money* fruicts: *fruits* binna: *apart from* ilka mait: *every meat, food* flair: *floor* unkent: *unknown* drave: *drove* thochts: *thoughts* agley: *aslant* muckle bounlessness: *huge boundlessness* ooriness: *eeriness* tuim howes: *empty hollows* souchin: *sighin (fricative ch)* brammles: *brambles* faurmaist mairches: *furthest bounds* lave: *remainder* feart: *afraid* fell an blinn: *cruel and blind*

FLICHTERIE WATHER

Grey Gallowa, green Gallowa:
the hulls smoort oot Carsphairn awa,
the smirrin wat blaws owre the muir
an thare's nae pleisure in't ava.

Green Gallowa, grey Gallowa:
the wrack's aw gane, the lift is skyre
and wastlins ower Merrick Tap
a burnist tairge o gowden fire.

PRIDE MAUN HAE A FAA

Thon bonnie peacock up et the Big Hoose
wad pace the green wi his lang fedders spreid,
his staurie tail gey near sax feet abreid.
Hou braw he wes, hou braw he wes an crouse,
nae coorse-lik orra burd had claes sae sprush.
Proodlie he bure the wee croun on his heid,
the wale o corn an meal-mash for his feed . . .
o the graund gentry thare the maist fantoosh.

Ochon a ri! A metamorphosis
o aa yon muckle pride hes cam his road;
oor michtie burd hes taen a hummle faa.

---

flichterie wather: *changeable weather* hulls: *hills* smoort oot: *smothered out* smirrin wat: *misty rain* wrack: *broken cloud* lift: *sky* skyre: *crystal clear* wastlins: *westwards* tairge: *a shield*

wale: *choice* ochon a ri: *alas*

Yae forenicht thro the Big Hoose rose-busses
thare cam on him a scabbit, hungert tod.
Nou he's twa tollies doun the birkenshaw.

THE SIMMERS PASS

The gress growes still sae caller green
ablo the bourtree's bloom,
tho halflin dwaums are langsyne flown
lik blossom frae the broom.

Braw nou the petal on the buss,
strang brainch abune ma heid,
but slaw the fuit on simmer pads
whaur yince I made guid speed.

---

tod: *fox* tollies: *turds*

simmer: *summer* caller: *fresh* ablo: *below* bourtree: *elder* halflin: *stripling* dwaums: *dreams* langsyne: *long ago* braw: *handsome* buss: *bus* pads: *paths* yince: *once*

A HANDFUL OF SILVER

There was a ruddy rebel man
who could not love a lord,
or such as kept their riches
with a curtain wall and sword,
so he kept on shooting at the moon.

'I care not if they torture me
with thumbscrew, boot or branks;
I'll never bend a coward knee
to give such robbers thanks,
so I'll keep on shooting at the moon.'

But digging in his cabbage plot
his spade clinked on a chest;
he gave a coin for charity
then hoarded all the rest,
and he winked and blew a kiss up to the moon.

SUIBHNE 'SA MHADAINN

Dùisg! arsa Suibhne,
a' cur a thaic ri ceann mo leaba;
bha thu raoir air iteal dìreach cho math rium fhein.
Facail sgiathach, àrd-shunndach, glòrach,
is do ghairdein a' sìor-luasgadh.

Cha b'e gu robh thu 'nad ruith air falbh
bho thaibhsean uamhasach 'san iarmailt,
bho bhraighdeanas dhaoine deagh-rùnach;
is ann a bha thu a' teagasg
feallsanachd, sgoilearachd, diadhachd;
a' tilgeil salmadair an lochan an inntinn
is a' daoibhig 'na dheidh fo uisge tana 'ga shaoradh,
's tu gun eisdeachd ri gealtairean eile.

A nisd, mar a rinn mi fhein,
ìthidh thu bracaist bhon dunan;
peanas an fheadhainn a dh'fheuchas
sòlas gun naomhachd.

Dùisg! arsa Suibhne,
le braoisg eagalach air a chlàb . . .
is mithich dhuit eìrigh . .
is do chasan critheanach circe sìos air làr.

SWEENEY IN THE MORNING*

Wake up! says Sweeney,
leaning on the end of my bed.
Last night you were flying just as well as myself;
great winged ecstatic, high-sounding words
and your arms forever waving.

It wasn't that you were running away
from horrid spectres in the heavens
or the restrictions of well-meaning friends.
You were busy teaching philosophy, scholarship, theology,
throwing a psalter into the loch of their minds
and diving into the shallow water
to rescue it and never listening
to any of the other poltroons.

Now, as I did myself,
you will eat breakfast from the dungheap,
the penance of those who attempt
enlightenment without holiness.

Wake up! says Sweeney
with a fearful grin on his gob.
It's high time you were up . . .
and your shivering chicken's legs down on the floor.

---

* Suibhne (Sweeney) is the Suibhne of the ancient Gaelic legend, Suibhne Geilt, nothing to do with T.S. Eliot!

FIRST KEEK AT A CORP

I mind the sicht o the auld wife's face begrutten
et Big Wull's daith an ma faither gane frae hame,
an me the bairn wha hud the deid man's name.
Come ben, they said, *come ben afore he's pitten
in his lang hame, come ben nou whan ye're bidden
ti pey yir lest respecks; he lukks the same
as aye he did.* The coffin like a frame
limned oot the corp, aw in the linins hidden.

But no the face. Twesna the man I kent,
weel loed bi bairns an dugs, an auld yins tae.
Ma tears cam no for this but the myndit man.

No this auld menseless corp, cauld, wan an spent,
shuin ti be yirdit in its mither clay.
I wesna muckle fasht whaur yon wes gaun.

BERRIES

Slae o the bleckthorn
afouth on the tree,
ye pit me in mind
o a tink limmer's ee,
wha langsyne in hairst
med a gowk oot o me.

---

ben: *inside* lang hame: *grave* menseless: *senseless* yirdit: *buried* muckle fashed: *greatly worried*

slae: *sloe* afouth: *in abundance* tink limmer: *tinker hussy* langsyne: *long ago* hairst: *harvest* gowk: *fool*

O straucht spirlie rowan
sae dern in the wuid,
the berries drap doun
aff yir brainches lik bluid
frae the herts that no langsyne
sae near ye were laid.

O braid bussie bourtree
yir flooers are aa gane,
yir leaf flitters doun nou,
yir berries are taen,
an the brainch souchs abune
as I walk here ma lane.

PRUDENCE

Walkin this mornin by anither loch
glaizie wi ice ablo an early sun,
I mindit the first day that I wes brocht
by bigger bairns doun tae the Laundry Pown.
Rin doun the hull, they said, an tear et it;
(they maun hae keeked and nidged et yin anither)
an I sclimt up richt tae the tapmaist bit
an skelpin doun cam I withooten swither.
Syne straucht I duntit doun on ma bit airse
an no a saicont later on ma heid;
ma skraichs an yells an black-begrutten face
shuin tellt the ithers that I wesna deid.

---

straucht: *straight* spirlie: *slim* dern: *hidden* bussie bourtree: *bushy elder tree* souchs: *sighs*

glaizie: *glossy* pown: *pond* keeked: *winked* sclimt: *climbed* skelpin: *racing* swither: *indecision* duntit: *thumped* skraichs (hard ch): *yells* begrutten: *tear-stained*

But no the day; I cawd a muckle stane . . .
it sklifft alang the ice; it didna brek . .
I shauchled oot a yaird and back again. . . .
nou leirit tae be cannie like the feck.

Wyce bairns shuin lairn; sair airses an split heids
smoor oot the gust fir owre-heroic deeds.

CROWD CONTROL DUTY

Soldiering then I seldom thought of gods,
only of girls, and didn't care a damn.
Armour, weapon and tactic framed the odds;
marshals, not gods, drilled us in battle plan.
As for the enemy, if he stood or ran,
our lines retreat in order or advance . .
weather or weariness might tilt the chance.

Detailed to stand in a provincial street
I leaned against the shoving, heard the crowd
yell for their holiday thrill, their annual treat.
I watched the prisoner stagger with head bowed
bloody of back beneath the gallows-load.
A sudden sharpness of eye told me the man
outstripped in grace the gaudy pantheon.

---

sklifft: *scraped* shauchled: *shambled* leirit: *taught* feck: *the majority* smoor: *smother*

FEIDH

An raoir, mar a gheall an sanas,
bha na feidh air an rathad,
sùilean lainnireach an solus a' chàr.
Cha b'iad na feidh ruadha nam beann àrda
ach an fheadhainn beag a th' againn sa choilltean Ghallobha.
Thanaig sreath bàrdachd Dhonnchaidh 'nam inntinn:
'Chunnaic mi 'n dàmh donn sna h-eildean . . .'

Cha tigeadh dhomhsa ach facail bheaga 'na choimeas
mu na feidh bheaga seo:
'Ma 's beag iad, tha iad grinn is neo-challaichte,
agus, gus an tig an saoghal gu crìoch,
dìleas d'an ghnè-san.'

DEER

Last night, as the sign promised,
the deer were on the road,
shining eyes in the car's light.
These were not the red deer of the high mountains,
but the little ones we have in the woods of Galloway.
A line of Duncan's poetry came into my mind:
'I saw the brown stag and his hinds . .'

Nothing would come to me but little words compared to his,
about these little deer:
'If they are small, they are graceful and untamed
and, till their world comes to an end,
faithful to their kind.'

TREE SPEIK

Dae they mind on us, the trees, in the grey touns
whaur a tree is anither thing in a Cooncil Park
lik a widden bink, aw thir tame beds o flouers
in couthie suburbs hapt wi an airn dyke,
nae mair a pairt o their realitie
nor fremit beasts in a faur ceetie zoo?
Are we kent as trees ainlie when the mind's tuim
an the hairns sined oot frae the warld's wechtie daurg?
No sib tae the ettlin warld whaur they bide. . . .
the warld o transport, television an tea-time,
or seen merely as naitural conveniences
a bonnie backgrunn tae the kintra picnic.

---

mind on: *remember* widden bink: *wooden bench* thir: *these* couthie: *comfortable* hapt: *wrapped, surrounded* airn dyke: *iron fence* fremit: *strange, foreign* tuim: *empty* hairns sined oot: *brainwashed* sib tae: *related to* ettlin: *busy trying* kintra: *country*

Whit dae they ken o the time we fullt *Coed Celyddon*
bussin the glens frae Kentigern's Green Place . .
frae Clyde tae Solway shore.

A man micht gae for weeks in the tree's shade
an nivir staund ablo the selsame brainch.
Dae they wha bide in Suibhne's Gallowa
or whaur yince stuid the forests o Srath-Chluaidh
ken whaur under the braid bield o trees
lane Lailocen walkit wud, there Taliesin,
Bluchbard and Cian sang tae the Northern Men,
listenin aye listenin tae the souch
heich in the brainch o aiks . .
auld whan oor laund wes young.

We are the *darach* and *derwen*
the druids honoured in the aiken-shaw;
they yaised oor michtie herts withooten greed,
takkin but the needit portion, kennin
that learit tent maun be taen o lievin things:
for trees, as men an beasts are lievein things;
the board an plank the bare banes o a corse.

Ken we are fauldit intil Scottish lear
tae mak a Gaelic alphabet o trees:
Ailm, Beithe,
Coll, Darach, Eadha, Fearn
Iubhar.

---

fullt: *filled* Coed Celyddon: *The ancient Forest of Caledonia (Welsh)* bussin: *dressing*
bide: *stay* yince: *once* Strath-Chluaidh: *Strathclyde (Gaelic)* bield: *shelter* lane: *lone*
wud: *mad* souch: *sigh* heich: *high* aiks: *oaks* darach, derwen: *oaks (Gae. and*
Welsh) aiken-shaw: *oakwood* yaised: *used* learit tent: *educated attention* corse: *corpse*
lear: *learning*

An we are different as men are different
frae yin anither, frae aw ither beasts,
the aik is no the elm . . nor yae brainch lik anither.
Wha kens us nou forbye the forester
tellin wi a glisk o the ee
The Mither o Forests frae the greetin sauchs;
the bonie rowan frae hir neebor hawbuss
hinging wi berries bi a burn in hairst?
Wha kens the simmer shade o the heich brainch
the leafie shaddas o the forest croun?

Een the sicht o the bare winter birk, aik, elm
kin heize the spierit, bare o aw foilyie still
the warrantie o flouer-buskit spring,
when snawdrap, daff an wund-flouer growe ablo
an leaf on brawest leaf we burgeon tae the simmer
in *breacan* setts o ilka green an siller . .
an oor green haunds raxin oot yin til ither
till hairst caas doon the simmers bonie cloak
tae lay a carpet on the forest flair
that the maist eident wabster couldna mak.

We are the bonie trees o the teuch hert
treisure tae the square-wricht's skeelie haund,
an nou as jimp as gowd. We are the trees
that bieldit the wild boar.
Whaur is yon craiter nou?

---

yae: *one* glisk: *glance* ee: *eye* greetin sauchs: *weeping willows* hawbuss: *hawthorn*
birk: *birch* heize: *uplift* foilie: *foliage* wund-flouer: *anemone* ablo: *below* brawest:
most handsome breacan (Gae): *tartan* ilka: *each, every* raxin: *reaching* eident
wabster: *diligent weaver* teuch: *tough* square-wricht: *carpenter of furniture* skeelie:
skilful jimp: *scarce* bieldit: *sheltered*

An as the boar hes gane, sae crine oor neebor trees
an gin the seedlin isna gart tae growe,
sae man will tine oor saucht an michtie bield.

nor twa hunner year, ten o yir generations
fill oot the lifetime o the noble aik;
yon souchin brainch heich abune Doon an Nith
bieldit the heid o men whae talked wi Burns.

Pit back the trees that med the birkenshaw,
the wuids o eild, the lang braid, dochtie forest
o aik and elm and *faibhile*,
that busked the straths langsyne.

Pit back the aik, the rowan an the sally
see yince again the blackthorn on the druim;
rowan an elm, the birk an bonie gean
for as our ruits haud tae yir native yird
sae mankind staunds,
an as we faa tae nocht sae mankind faas,
an the haill mapamound
crines tae a steirless craig withooten saul,
whaur the suin's licht
faas on the bieldless stour o a beld stern.

---

crine: *wither* gart: *compelled* tine: *lose* saucht: *peaceful* souchin: *sighing* birkenshaw: *birchwood* eild: *the past, former times* dochtie: *sturdy* faibhile (Gae): *beech* busked: *dressed* straths: *river valleys* langsyne: *long ago* sally: *willow* yince: *once* druim: *hill-ridge* birk: *birch* gean: *wild cherry* yird: *earth* nocht: *nothing* haill mapamound: *whole sphere of the world* crines: *withers* steirless craig: *unstirring rock* beld stern: *bald star*

CLAONAIG

(Air son Deorsa Caimbeul Hay nach maireann)

Air traigh Chlaonaig Chinntire
coimhead a rithisd air cìr Arainn,
cha robh togail 'nam chrìdhe
air son boidhchead an fhearainn.

Chaidh mo chas air a' ghainneamh
'san dùthaich bu ghnàth leat,
far an diugh is glè ainneamh
a chluinnear sreath Gàidhlig.

Guth do bhàrdachd an lathair
far an d'shoirbhich do lèirsinn
roimh eilthireachd 'sa Chathair
is là falamh do thrèigsinn.

Anns an t-seòmar beag caol
aig a cheann thall do theinne,
ged bu chùl leat ri gaoth
dh'fhalbh ort teas na greine.

CLAONAIG

(For the late George Campbell Hay)

On the beach of Claonaig in Kintyre
looking again on the comb of Arran
there was no lifting in my heart
at the beauty of the land.

My foot went on the sand
of the country you knew
where now it is seldom
one hears a phrase of Gaelic.

The voice of your poetry was there
where your insight prospered
before the exile of the City
and the empty day of your betrayal.

In the little narrow room
at the far end of your strife,
though your back was to the wind
the heat of the sun deserted you.

STIOPALL ULM

*Stad an trèan air an drochaid.
Chunnaic mi stiopall Ulm ag èirigh
àrd, àrd, san iarmailt soilleir glan
mar obair-ghrèis air aodach gorm neimhe;
dualan Ceilteach san adhair.*

*Gun teagamh, thanaig an smuain sin a stigh
air iomadh fògarrach Gaidhealach
sna ceudan fada dh'aom
is cuimhne aca air Alba
nan dualan imfhillte.
Manaich, sgoilearan, saighdearan..
prìomh marsantachd na h-Alba.*

*Gu h-obann bha iad ann,
is b'aithne dhomh iad.
Chòrd an cuideachd sin na b'fheàrr rium
na fàileasan bàna mo latha-sa
air cabhsairean mo dhùthcha
is iad an imcheist
mu'n dualchas aca.*

THE SPIRE OF ULM

The train stopped on the bridge.
I saw the spire of Ulm rising
high, high into the clear bright firmament,
like lacework on the blue garment of heaven;
Celtic patterns in the sky.

Doubtless that thought had come
to many an exiled Gael
in the long centuries that have gone
and they remembering Scotland
of the entwined patterns.
Monks, scholars, soldiers . .
Scotland's chief exports.

Suddenly they were there
and I recognised them.
I found their company more congenial
than the pale shadows of my own day
on the pavements of my country
and they uncertain
of their own heritage.

KIRKS SUDNA BE OWRE BRAID

MacCowal wes brocht up in The Nerra Kirk,
that, Setternicht, stowed cocks ablo a creel,
an cleekt up the weans' swings an birlin-wheel,
an awkin ither barebaned godlie wark
thay thocht wad shuin ding doun the Pouers o Daurk.
Nou, growne tae man's estait he canna feel
sic ootlan weys will hain him frae The Deil
the day he's laid trig in his yirdin-sark.

Nou he's be gleg in onie kirk or nane:
synagogue, mosque, pagoda, Quauker Hoose,
The Kirk o Joukerie-Poukerie, or Plain Sailin.

Staunch pillars o aw sects syne tell him plain:
sauls athoot spiecial kirks sud no be crouse;
aw heresie growes frae a want o walin.

Nerra Kirk: *narrow church* Setternicht: *Saturday night* creel: *peat-basket* cleekt up: *locked up* weans: *children* birlin-wheel: *roundabout* awkin: *all kinds of* shuin: *soon* ding doun: *knock down* hain: *preserve* trig: *neat* yirdin-sark: *burial shirt* gleg: *joyous* Joukerie-Poukerie: *jiggery-pokery* syne: *then* athoot: *without* crouse: *happy* walin: *choosing*

STARS

Standing beneath the heaven here alone
I see the stars like jewels on velvet lie
in the same figures I have always known
in all my years below the curving sky.
Tonight a coldness lies upon my heart,
their beauty does not charm as it did then,
a child, when neither reasoning nor art
coaxed me to one or other school of men
or later faction when I thought them wise.
The grain is shaken from my sheaf of years
the stars are fading in my seeking eyes,
there is no music in the distant spheres;
they tell the truth about all things that are:
nothing, o nothing stays, not one clear diamond star.

INFERNO

Thir Malebolges gar ye sweit a taet;
nestie, frae Circle Yin tae Circle Nine,
een fur wee tottie sleekit fauts lik mine.
Whummlin aroon in yon infernal pit
that gowps doun hoor an bellygut an wit
maks deity luk a wee thing less benign.
Cairds, houghmagandie, mockery o wine . . .
thir hellish thochts tak aa the pleisure fae't.

Thir: *these* gar: *make* sweit: *sweat* taet: *a little bit* yin: *one* wee tottie: *miniscule*
sleekit: *sly* faut: *fault* whummlin: *whirling about* gowp: *gulp* hoor: *whore* bellygut: *glutton* Cairds: *cards* houghmagandie: *fornication* fae't: *from it*

But then, o coorse, in oor enlichtent day
wha lippens tae yon hellfire an damnation,
the brunstane reek, rettle o chine an fetter?

An whan ye stert tae think on aa the weys
mankind's inventit for pain's coancentration
whit maks ye think the Deil cud dae it better?

---

lippens tae: *trusts to, credits* brunstane reek: *sulphurous smoke* rettle: *rattle*
chine: *chain*

CRAOBHAN

*Chuala mise gum b'urrainn dhaibh o shean
coiseachd fo chraobhan bho Chluaidh gu Solabhaigh;
a nisd chaneil a leithid de chraobhan againn . .
ach paireid reiseamaid ghiuthas air gach sliabh.*

*Is toigh leam gu bheil coille cheart air fhagail
eadar an Lochan Dubh is an Gleann Luachrach
gun duine ann ach mi fhein mar mhial na h-aonar
troimh bhachlag bheag saoghail a tha 'fàs maol.*

*A nisd on a tha iad a' bearradh claigeann an t-saoghail
is a' tarraing a mach ciabhagan uaine an domhain,
tha mi taingeil airson an t-sopain anns a bheil mi;
chaneil dìon ann idir le mial air ceann maol.*

TREES

I have heard that it was possible in days of old
to walk under trees from Clyde to Soìway;
now we don't have that amount of trees,
but a regimental parade of pines on every hillslope.

I am glad that there is a proper wood left
between the Black Loch and the Rushy Glen,
nobody there but myself like a louse on its own
through the small curl of a world that is growing bald.

Now, since they are shaving the skull of the world
and pulling out the green locks of the earth,
I'm grateful for the little wisp that I'm in.
There's no protection for a louse on a bald head.

GRIAN IS GEALACH

Thig e a stigh ort
aig ceann thall ar strì-ne
gur urrainn ain-tighearnas
la soilleir thoirt bhuainn.

Ged a dhallas a'ghrìan
sùil ag amharc a soillse,
is beò fhathast an cuimhne
gealach oirdheirc a raoir.

SUN AND MOON

It will come home to you
at the end of the struggle
that it is possible for injustice
to take the bright day from us.

But though the sun blinds
an eye that looks at its brightness,
the memory is alive still
of the splendid moon of yesterday.

CAOCHLADH

Uinneagan dubha air là grianach;
taigh 'sa bheil corp na h-òighe.
An deidh seachdainn le geall samhraidh,
fuar-ghaoth troimh chonnasg buidhe.

CHANGING*

Dark windows on a sunny day;
a house wherein is the corpse of a virgin.
After a week with the promise of summer
a cold blast through yellow gorse.

ERMINE

On the braeface the day I saw a stoat
scutterin ower frae yae dike til the tither,
weel happit up anent the winter weather
in a maist braw and gentie ermine coat
white as the yowdendrift withooten spot,
cosie and warm as lambs' woo unner laither
but hae'in yae advantage awthegither:
the claes whauron baith lairds and leddies dote.

Ye'll see thaim thair on monie a graund occasion
in gowden coronets; the beastie's skin
steekit in winter white on scarlet coat,
proodlie paradin there afore the nation.
*The stoat kens fine it will gae broun again;
ablo aw finerie a stoat's a stoat.*

---

* In Gaelic, 'changing' equals dying.

braeface: *hillside* scutterin: *scampering* dike: *hedge* yae: *one* happit: *wrapped* anent: *against* braw and gentie: *handsome and fine* yowdendrift: *drifting snow*

GEOIDH

*Air earrann rèidh, uaine, faisg air an loch an diugh
chunnaic mi na geòidh ag ionaltradh 'nan ceudan;
chuala iad guth an fhreiceadain is dh'èirich iad
le buillean làidir is ro-chùmhachd air sgiathan.*

*Tha mi gun fhios ciamar a ni iad eagair
gach aon dhiubh an dèidh a chèile gu lèir gun smuain;
chan fhada nis gus an till iad a rìthisd mu thuath;
gun chàirt-iùil no combaist theid iad dhan ceann-uidhe.*

*Ach, aig a cheann thall, chaneil eanchainn aca;
is e dùchas nàdurach a chumas iad bho chunnart.
Is e gibht phriseil dhaoine, lèirsinn is innleachd,
gun dùchas na geòidh 'gar dìonadh bho Mhòr-thubaist.*

GEESE

On flat green ground near the loch today
I saw the geese grazing in their hundreds;
they heard the call of the sentry and rose with a strong beat of powerful wings.

I do not know how they maneouvre, each one after its comrade entirely without thought;
not long now till they return again to the north; without chart or compass they will reach their goal.

But when all is said and done they have no brains;
it is merely instinct that keeps them from danger.
Insight and vision are the great gifts of mankind, without the nature of geese to protect us from disaster.

FASACH

Teas dùmhail feasgar Cheitinn
is an trean a snaigeadh thar Rainich
mar nathair 'na dùsgadh as ùr;
leabhar Dhonnchaidh na mo laimh.

Fear coshurtail mum choinneamh:
'Leugh mi sin o chionn fhada,
ach cha do mhothaich mi a dìth
sa Chuirt nam Morairean Dearg.
Foghnaidh beagan Laideann is Beurla Mòr.'

Sheall mi thar a' mhointich nam thòsd.
Bu chuimhne leam sean sgeul
gur e seo Aite nan Daoine Brìste.

WILDERNESS

The close heat of a May evening
and the train crawling over Rannoch
like a newly awakened adder:
The book of Duncan (Ban MacIntyre) in my hand.

A comfortable man opposite me:
'I read that a long time ago,
but I never noticed the lack of it
in the Court of the Red Lords (the law courts).
A little Latin and High English will suffice.'

I looked over the moor and kept silent.
I remembered the old story
that this was The Place of the Broken Men.

THE SONNET-GOLOCH

Bewaur yon Sonnet-Goloch; a sair stang
he'll gie, gin ye're no tentie whan ye read;
his venim kills aw ither vairse stane-deid:
Rime Royal, Auchtfauld Rime an sempil sang
nae maitter hou ye scan thaim soond aw wrang.
In dwams an wauken, birlin roon the heid
aw thocht is yerkit intil Petrarch's cleed
o fowerteen lines; an that's no ower lang.

He'll hap ye ticht in octet an sestet
bi faur the stievest o aw crambo-clink . . .
nae easie-osie moadern tapsalteerie.

Lowse frae his fanklin wab ye canna get . .
sae gin the Sonnet-Goloch ye wad jink
weir aff Daurk Leddies, Belli an Rab Garie.

Goloch: *beetle* sair stang: *sore sting* tentie: *careful* Auchtfauld Rime: *ottava rima* sempil: *simple* dwams: *dreams* birlin: *whirling* yerkit: *tightly bound* cleed: *garb* stievest: *stiffest* crambo-clink: *rhyming verse* easie-oasie: *lackadaisical* tapsalteerie: *chaotic* lowse: *loose* fanklin: *entangling* jink: *dodge* weir aff: *fend off* Rab Garie: *Robert Garioch (the correct pron.)*

FEASGAR FANN FOGHAIR

Eadar an Lùnasdal 's an Fhèill Martainn
le caoruinn sgarlaid a' fàs gu trom,
sgàthan an lochan gu lèir gun chaitean
feasgar fonn foghair is annsa leam.

Ceò 's an t-simileir ag eirigh direach,
smeuran dubha air an drìs nach gann;
ri taobh na h-aibhne mo shòlas-inntinn
feasgar fonn foghair is annsa leam.

Bagairt a' gheamhraidh le fuachd is fiadhaichead
is coma leam sin 'san uair a th'ann....
fèath 'san iarmailt is fèath 'nam chridhe;
feasgar fonn foghair is annsa leam.

A QUIET AUTUMN EVENING

Between Lammas and Martinmas
when the rowan berries hang heavily,
the mirror of the loch without a ripple . .
a quiet autumn evening is my delight.

Smoke rising straight from the chimney,
black berries on the bramble without scarcity;
my contentment is by the river . .
a quiet autumn evening is my delight.

The threat of winter with its cold and wildness . .
I couldn't care less about that just now . . .
calm in the heavens and calm in my heart;
a quiet autumn evening is my delight.

ANITHER BLEST O JANUAR WUN

Back yince again tae white-waashin Rab Burns.
A peetie tes thare's nane o thaim tak tent
o whit the haill shaif o his scrievins *meant*,
insteid o gien thir yearlie coamic turns
in speik faur mair weel-kent in Newton Mearns.
Goad, the haill ettle o the bard 's been bent
sae ilka thowless philistine kin pent
his 'Life of Burns' owre neaps, aitmeal-an-thairms.

---

yince: *once* tak tent: *pay attention* shaif: *sheaf* scrievins: *writings* speik: *speech* weel-kent: *well known* ettle: *intention* ilka: *each* pent: *paint* neaps: *turnips* aitmeal-an-thairms: *oatmeal and offal (haggis)*

Hear this yin nou, wha'd mak *his* Bard teetotal
spite o aw *reamin swats* an *usquebae*,
tippeny, pecks o maut an *pints o wine*.

Ye'd think Rab Burns had nivir seen a boattle.
Whit maitter? Yin wha med braw sangs lik thae,
gin he wes gey an tozie aw the time.

THE TRUER VISION

From the cell window past the prison gable
he saw the topmost branches of a tree;
watched them each day as long as he was able,
the only living freedom he could see.

His spirit failed him at the chainsaw's roar
on the grey morning that they cut it down;
till he recalled what had been there before,
and closed his eyes to watch its leafy crown.

OLD SCHOLAR

Fire flickers in the winter dusk;
the flames breathe in the chimney's throat
whispers of knowledge to the wise:
they know who know they know nothing.

---

reamin swats, usquebae, tippeny, pecks o maut, pints o wine: *descriptions of drink from Burns' own poems* thae: *those* gey an tozie: *fairly drunk*

Shadows have been his long companions
in ageless caverns of the mind,
more real to him than flesh and blood,
or blind time of the market place.

Pliny sits in the facing chair.
Odysseus repeats his yarns
of dark seas, shipwreck, fair women.
The pendulum wags out his life.

LIAM ON HIS SECOND BIRTHDAY

In the first grey light, quietly
you arose from restless sleep;
who was the greybeard in the other bed?
Did you recognise your ancestor
or is that a state that comes with time?
Love perhaps, later an estimation.

Seeing this other being
you bombarded it with a stuffed rabbit;
it made friendly noises,
this thing the world outside will call a grandfather,
but really just an older baby
who has found other toys than stuffed rabbits,
and, tired of these, bombarded the world with them.

As you will do, my grandson
if providence allows.

I hope that when your stuffed rabbit
hits the world on the head,
they will smile at you
as I did.

HILL AND CLOUD

Granite sparkle,
morning shine;
far mountains
firm of line.

Slim verse is
a sorry shift,
to catch high heaven's
stippled drift.

MINOR OPERATION

The surgeon tells me: *here's what I will do*;
(a slice he's taken many times before)
I visualise the knife, sinews and gore;
coward prognosis takes the gloomy view.

*If just by chance we should divide a nerve
you'll find a loss of feeling in the hand;
something that can't be helped you understand.* . . .
I wonder if numb finger-ends will serve.

Thin arms, slim waists that move my aging bulk
from bed to lift and trolley turn me over. . . .
sleep now, says one as gentle as a mother
serving nepenthe to my swimming hulk.

A pretty face looks down . . *Wake up* . . *wake up.*
How have I gained this Muslim paradise?
after my sins to merit smiling eyes. . . .
this theatre angel in a nurse's cap.

I lie, an arm suspended in the air
hopefully sterile, from its gallows beam;
easy and quiet now enough to seem
free from another difficult affair.

CARRION

A ragged crow rots, flapping on the wire,
hanged by the feet for brigand insolence.
Proud of his tricks, he mocked the flying shot,
kept out of range till age and greed betrayed him.
Now, like the plundered barley, head hangs down,
his strutting legs fettered by binder twine,
the carrion talons curled to empty air.

My beak points homeward cheerfully enough,
but his, more surely, like a compass needle
marks out the course to our common destination.

HIGH SQUADRONS

Bones of dead geese wait by the river's edge
to crumble earthwards and be raised again
as sinews of new captains flying north
in echelon formations beyond thought.

What more of life than in these noble squadrons
delighting in high flight upon the wind,
sigh of concealing reed and migrant urge;
what more of calmness than deep inland water,
promise of spring, sure wings above the strath?

A joyous miracle are wild birds voyaging
against the cloudless blue that holds their cry,
forging an instant of unthinking truth
caught yesterday, mirrored in the swans' pool,
not to be written down, or framed in speech.

MAKING TRACKS

Down the sloping face of the hill park
tractor ruts darken the soft green
that knew the kinder mark of boot and hoof.

Down the tanned face of the old watcher
who knew the horses and despised the tractor
the ruts of time give warrant to the memory.

RETOUR FRAE THE CITIE

The suin in azure heich alowe,
wild geese gane frae the watter-howe,
spring smoors oot winter's bane.
I wha in Edimbro wes pent
wi stanie biggins for ma stent
walk this braid muir alane.
Mair blythe nor this I couldna be
gin I were hained frae thocht,
faur ben in halie glamourie,
bricht luminous in Nocht;
but thocht's tine's no ma hine
when sicht an soun are thrang,
whaur bird sings an bud springs
the souchin shaws amang.

Thro craig an carse the watters rin,
breengin an skinklin in the suin
as hilltaps tine thair snaw.
The lambs lowp gleg on ilka knowe,
whaur caller green on howme and howe
busks landart's plaidie braw.
I luk doun frae this muirland heicht
on lochan, lea and burn,
a brechan-sett ablo ma sicht
ilk airt I chaise tae turn.
I ken fine in spring time
the gait that I wad be.
I peetie the ceetie,
Here bides true majestie.

---

retour: *return* heich alowe: *high blazing* watter-howe: *water-hollow* smoors: *smothers* biggins: *buildings* stent: *support* gin I were hained: *if I were saved* glamourie: *enchantment* tine: *loss* hine: *place, haven* thrang: *busy* souchin shaws: *sighing woods* craig: *rock* carse: *flat ground by a river* breengin (soft *g*): *rushing violently* skinklin: *shimmering* tine: *lose* lowp gleg: *leap lively* ilka knowe: *each hillock* caller: *fresh* howme: *holm* busks: *decorates* landarts: *landward, landscape* brechan-sett: *tartan pattern* ilk airt: *each way* gait: *road, way*

DRUMLIE DAY

A blashie day an smirr doun on the Rinns;
the simmer bides awa for aw the green.
I gove atour the muir an coont ma sins,
sichin for the wechtie deeds I micht hae duin.

An no yae wather-gleam tae heize the maitter;
a menseless, mirkie day o mochie gloom,
whan the lift's luggies are lippen-fu o watter,
an Goad alane kens whan they'll aw be tuim.

SEASCAPE

The weekend sailors tried to come alongside,
drylanders to a man; the old men watched
too shy to offer help, then one spoke out.
The chief of bunglers talked of kedging off,
looked down his nose: *It's all right, we can manage.*
Another fathom out, said Calum Do'laidh,
and the tide will take them all a trip to Ireland.

Old Erchie leaned against his upturned boat.
Just something to pass the time, scraping and painting.
I offered him the caulking of his seams;
he wiped his whiskers, nodded towards the kyle.
Maybe next time she'll take me out to join
my brothers lying yonder off the sgeir.

---

drumlie: *clouded/troubled* blashie: *drenching* smirr: *misty drizzle* gove: *glower* sichin: *sighing* wechtie: *weighty* wather-gleam: *light on the horizon* heize the maitter: *uplift the matter/improve things* menseless: *senseless* mirkie: *dark* mochie: *muggy* lift: *sky* luggies: *milking pails* lippen-fu: *brimming over* kens: *knows* tuim: *empty*

STRAIGHT LINES

GILLESPIE'S WOOD

Bright Monday and I walking
from the black croft to the rushy glen,
under the shade of trees by the riverside,
grass growing freshly in the wood-clearings,
calm in the heavens and on the river-pool,
everything under the quiet of early spring,
and my eye often on each hill crowned
with a gleam of late winter snow.

The white swan and his faithful lover
swim stately by on the smooth mirror,
the snowdrop spread on every bank
and the daffodil coming to bloom.
A gentle man is Gillespie,
who will kill no creature for sport;
each bird and beast with the way of its kind
and I one with all creation.

Standing at peace among these trees,
oak and birch, yew and beech,
that started many a year before me
and grew free from bite of saw or axe;
my hope—they wave loftily
their noble branches in the clear sky
many a long year over the head of Gillespie,
who saved the crown of the forest for us.

HOME THOUGHTS IN THE PIAZZA

We were remote and running on scythed wheels,
when these were polished, regular, urbane,
between the *altopiano* and the plain
where Dante's compeers rigged their daggered schemes.

Sweet-sounding strings, under an evening sky
smooth as shot silk above the colonnade.
Where mercenaries marched and Caesar played,
we sit and sip within a warm wind's sigh.

On our wet moorland, by their last frontier,
brown water rages white through scattered stone;
this, our first sculpture, carved by time alone,
stubbornly in our vision even here.

THE MILLMAN

October's moon over the evening yard,
rumble of wheels upon the rutted road,
breaking the earth, for all the frost was hard
under that iron load.

Steam tractor, threshing mill and caravan
come there to part their straw and chaff and grain,
the final fruiting of the peasant plan,
reward of labour's pain.

Into the firelit room the millman came,
with a hook for a hand, a face as pale as death;
the child, who saw all grown men as the same,
drew in a frightened breath.

The millman only grinned and waved his hook,
stuck down his corpse's face to the boy's head:
I'm more alive, my laddie, than I look.
It's just my hand that's dead. . . .

and buried too, for it was never found
when the engine skidded on the bank and fell.
I often sit and think about that hand,
waiting in heaven or hell.

MS DICKINSON (1830-1886)

Think of bright Emily sitting quietly there
in her lone room, arrayed in virgin white,
a metaphor that fitted her aright.
High Poetry was much more her affair,
though dull male editors could hardly bear
to read her verses; their opinion quite
that knitting or embroidery was the height
of Art permissible in female care.

Needlepoint frames could not contain the writer;
other designs she had, despite those males.
Knowing posterity would well requite her,
wrapped in brown paper all her nightingales
with sure and neat instructions for a brighter
posthumous generation, rising sales.

MULL FERRY

O fair young Mairead, love has wounded me,
O fair young lass with eyes as dark as sloes. . . .

We should have booked much earlier:
the car deck's absolutely packed.

The silver salmon I would take for you,
rich venison upon the hills of Mull . . .

The scenery's marvellous, those hills and things.
But the people! A depressing lot.

Eyes clear as dewdrops hanging from the branch,
so blue and still in the early morn. . . .

The important things, of course,
all run by people like ourselves.

O fair young Mairead, were I only there
in the high mountains of Mull with you. . . .

NEIL MACVURICH'S LOST POEMS

After the generations passed,
his seed, lowered from bards to tailors,
found the old vellum lying in a chest.

History robbed them of learning
in their own ancient tongue.
No harm it seemed to them
to cut up hide in tapes to measure cloth.

Be sparing of your sneers.
They could not read.
Blame those who read
and smother poets with a boor's indifference.

SEAL WOMEN

Remember in the taking of seal women
how such wild beauties were constrained to stay:
their cast hides seized by mortals, stowed away,
although their briny souls denied them heaven.

Being in the end the merest magical beasts,
despite silk skin, soft eyes and flowing hair.
Yet their desertion left an aching there,
when seas won back from men their secret breasts.

SINGING

It was seldom calm; most nights the usual wind
from Ireland across the machair, but no rain.
I walked in those light nights to the halfway inn
to drink myself singing. English words faded
as the night wore on. A body could believe
the song would never die in spite of all.

Homeward in that late twilight; abbey walls
rose to the skyline on the further island.
Surely their songs were holier far than ours,
bawled out in drink in yon rough hostelry?

But lonely there upon the morning shore,
knowing that in those taproom choruses
there was a yearning deep as sanctity.

SO FAIR A FANCY

What would you say if I should tell you all
I saw upon the hill the other night:
an angel sitting on a drystone wall,
his pinions gleaming in a mystic light?

A sight that poor Tom Hardy never saw,
but wished he had; the Immanence of Will
smacks of a granite Scientific Law,
not like my angel sitting on a hill.

If I should swear it on my mother's grave
you'd hesitate to say I was a liar,
but send for a psychiatrist to save
my head from harm, if not my soul from fire.

Ah well, I didn't see one, any more
than Tommy Hardy saw at Christmas time
the oxen kneeling on the stable floor
and put his longings on a bonny rhyme.

I thought it worth my while to tell a lie
that made your life less boring. My romance
sprang from the mood that made Tom Hardy sigh;
hope against hope we hadn't lost the chance.

TWO BLACK FINGERS

The other day I passed a slaughtered crow.
Undone at last by his too-urgent greed
he lay with funeral plumage all unfurled
and mocked from this last nest the ancient foe.
Since wingless we remain for all our speed,
two feathers raised, like fingers, to the world.

UNREGENERATE

Holyman came to call me to those old ways
that I won free of after many a year,
having lost all faith now in the way he prays,
demanding help for favour of love, or fear.

Last night again I almost worshipped the moon,
standing so full and fair above the clouds,
but men will build cathedrals up there soon,
say new selenic prayers to dodge their shrouds.

Missing the point. The moon's worth looking at
just for that still moment that is forever.
The earth is beautiful whether it's round or flat.
Holyman's prayers have grown too long, too clever.

WILD THINGS

Last night the woods were empty of humankind;
whispering trees, the gloaming cry of birds,
the flashing speckle of a startled hind,
but no shouts, no words.

Today the hounds bell over far fields,
wild things rush out from the shotgun's rattle,
the gun dogs wait till bid at their masters' heels,
keen for the battle.

UNCOLLECTED POEMS

BONNIE ARRAN

Frae an auld Gaelic poem scrievit aboot 100 AD.

Beluvit Arran o the nobil hynds
on yir braid shouthers braks the landbrist aye,
bonnie lang island whaur the kemps finn mait,
an whaur the lyart heids o speirs turn ridd.

Heich bens ootstreikit faur abuin the sea;
a walth of flours upo yon growthie greens,
braw nowte an horse in ilka park an shaw
an fouth o fowk atour the heich muir skailt.

the broun stag rairin on the tapmaist craig
blaeberries growe abreid on the braid muirs,
lipfu o caller watter, breengin burns ..
nuits bi the gowpen ben the aiken shaws.

Monie the grews thare an the huntin dugs;
the brammle, slae-buss an the jaggie thorn,
weel-foundit biggins bi the forest mairch
whaur the deer byde ablo the brainchin trees.

---

shouthers: *shoulders* landbrist: *breakers* kemps: *heroes, champions* mait: *meat, food* lyart: *grey* ridd: *red* heich bens: *high mountains* ootstreikit: *outstretched* growthie greens: *fertile swards* nowte: *cattle* ilka: *each, every* shaw: *wood* fouth: *abundance* atour: *across* skailt: *scattered* craig: *rock* blaeberries: *bilberries* abreid: *widespread* caller: *fresh* breengin: *charging forward (as a horse)* gowpen: *double handful* aiken shaws: *oak woods* grews: *greyhounds* brammle: *blackberry* slae-buss: *sloe-bush* biggins: *buildings* mairch: *boundary* byde: *stay, live*

Abuin the craigs the bonnie crottal growes,
gress athoot smit atour the growan green,
nae muirland thare athoot its ain bien bield,
an lowpin truit on ilka lochan splounge.

On lang flet machairs ligg the sonsie swine,
the nuit-brae falloch bi the hazel shaw,
faur doun the wuids the maumie aipples hing;
ablo ilk ness the buskit birlins ligg.

Blythesome ilk airt whan the bricht simmer cams
fush liggin bi the bank o loch an burn,
abuin the lyart scaurs the sea-maws skraich
o bonnie Arran, weel-beluvit aye.

---

crottal: *lichen* smit: *blemish* bien: *comfortable* bield: *shelter* lowpin: *leaping* lochan: *lakelet* splounge: *plunge* sonsie: *plump* falloch: *thickly heaped* maumie: *mellow* buskit birlins: *decorated galleys* ligg: *lie* airt: *place* scaurs: *cliffs* maws: *mews* skraich (ch as in 'loch'): *screech* aye: *always*

POETS' LOANINS

Daunner roon ony wee Italian toun
Gey near on ilka street thare's a stane heid
o some deid bard whase daurg in poetrie gied
warrant tae pit his honoured name abune
the Via Pascoli, or some ither loon
weel kent for sangs or duans. It's gey hard
for ony hamebound Caledonian bard
tae ken richt weill the ainlie names *he'll* finn.

Cooncillor Mucklewame an aa his kynd
are med immortal whan ye see the name
Mucklewame Terrace or MacPlitter's Pend.

Ye scart yir heid ettlin tae bring tae mind
what wes't that gied *thaim* sic a meid o fame.
Och, muve tae Italy gin ye'd be kenned.

---

loanins: *lanes* ilka: *every* daurg: *labour* abune: *above* loon: *fellow* duans: *verses, poems* pend: *archway to a back court* scart: *scratch* ettlin: *trying*